Lessons in Law Enforcement

Essential Tips From A Savvy DownEaster

YORK COUNTY
1636
FIRST COUNTY

By
Paul Main

Note for Librarians: A cataloguing record for this book is available from Library and Archives
Canada at www.collectionscanada.ca/amicus/index-e.html
ISBN 1-4251-0789-3

PUBLISHING™
Offices in Canada, USA, Ireland and UK

Book sales for North America and international:
Trafford Publishing, 6E–2333 Government St.,
Victoria, BC V8T 4P4 CANADA
phone 250 383 6864 (toll-free 1 888 232 4444)
fax 250 383 6804; email to orders@trafford.com
Book sales in Europe:
Trafford Publishing (UK) Limited, 9 Park End Street, 2nd Floor
Oxford, UK OX1 1HH UNITED KINGDOM
phone +44 (0)1865 722 113 (local rate 0845 230 9601)
facsimile +44 (0)1865 722 868; info.uk@trafford.com
Order online at:
trafford.com/06-2547

10 9 8 7 6 5 4 3

PREFACE

I would like to thank my dear friend Retired FBI Agent Jim Moores for encouraging me to do this project. Jim is a man I would trust with my wallet, my wife or my life. As a police officer you meet many people in the performance of you duty. I can honestly say that I have never met a better man or a more professional law enforcement officer than Jim Moores.

Thanks Jim, this one's for you.

This book is dedicated to the next generation of young people who have set their sights on a career in Law Enforcement. Most agencies today require a minimum of an Associate Degree to be considered for a position. The times are changing. Associates Degrees and computer knowledge are wonderful things and worthy of study. They're both real handy if a career is to be spent within the confines of a classroom.

My intent, is not to diminish new technology but to illustrate that the real classroom is not in a college or police academy but in life itself. I must confess that I have been guilty of unleashing my humor on some of the members of this new, unsuspecting generation. After all, college tells them, you can trust another cop. WRONG.

So, you want to be a cop. Well, I shall try to open your eyes about the real world of Law Enforcement. If just one reader gains any insight then this undertaking shall have been worth the effort. Police work is a great way of life, not a job. The real trick is the method by which it is approached.

The secret to success is really quite simple. Don't take yourself too seriously, but take the profession seriously, and maintain a controlled sense of humor.

Law Enforcement is about serving the public, not about you.

In my opinion, of all the qualities that a good Police Officer should possess, observation is the most important. I'm going to attempt to share some of my experiences in this book and you, the reader, can judge for yourself the quality that is most important.

CONTENTS

The Academy

Every police officer has to attend the police academy to earn the right to wear the uniform. That is, as it should be. However, an understanding of the goals and objectives brings the experience into proper focus. This is best described by breaking down academy time period into three segments.

The first third is designed to get rid of the Twits, or at least, most of them. The harassment and constant hazing of the Cadres usually gets the job done.

The real objective is to test the resolve of the cadet. The Cadres use physical and psychological measures to accomplish the task of Weeding Out.

I recall my academy days very clearly. I was one of the older cadets and had already been working a patrol schedule for a while prior to the Academy. I saw a few ex-servicemen walk out the door and quit. Well, the mindset is different from the military. The Cadres make it really clear that the Cadet isn't wanted and they take every opportunity to invite you to leave.

During the first few weeks, the physical demands are designed to develop you physically and stress you to the max emotionally. One of the methods they used was to keep you in the classroom on Fridays after the designated time when Cadets were permitted to leave for home for the weekend.

I recall the Cadre asking question about the range of topics that had been presented in classes that week. The questions were designed as related to, but beyond the material covered in class.

An incorrect response from a cadet brought ridicule from the cadre. All the while, keeping the Cadets from going home. Well to me, this was a declaration of a battle of wits. The fact that both Cadres were Troopers, basically told me that I was picking on unarmed people. (They're really good police officers but you just don't tell them that.)

I would return home, armed with the class syllabus for the up-coming week.

Saturday morning, I traveled to the County Courthouse and went to the law library. There I would research case law related to the next week's class and prepare a few select questions related to the several subjects. All my questions were on cases that were yet to be decided by the U. S. Supreme Court. In short, questions without answers.

I'd return for another week and during the next Friday Witching Hour, I laid in the weeds waiting. All I had to do was wait long enough and the opening would come. I'd ask one of the questions to the Cadre. Bear in mind that the Cadre wouldn't know a law library from a two-hole outhouse. It was absolutely the best feeling in the world to watch the man stumble around, hem and haw for ten minutes and say nothing or provide a 100 proof bullshit answer. Always followed by class dismissed!

Years later, a classmate, now working for the FBI, related to a dear friend of mine, who also worked in the FBI, that he recalled that I used to ask questions of the Cadres on Fridays when everyone wanted to go home. The sad part is my friend had to explain to my old classmate; (a), what I was doing and (b), it was always followed by class dismissed. You be the judge.

Oh, incidentally, it only took four weeks before we got to leave on time and on graduation day I told the Cadres that there were no correct answers to the questions. Justice is sweet.

The second phase is the classroom and group psychology period. This is what I called the Bob Barker time because I watched classmates jockey for position, as class officers were elected. The only thing that came to my mind was " COME ON DOWN; you could be the next contestant on The Price Is Right."

This is when the true education really begins. You get to see what people will do for a title. The fact is nobody gives a hoot in hell who the class president is during the academy or five minutes after graduation. But the journey is worth watching.

Each class is given a number for identity. So the race begins with what the class will leave for a mark at the academy. Well, here's where that most important attribute, observation, comes into play. Just about any third grade kid could look around the dining hall and see that the walls were plastered with class photos. That should be a strong hint of the tradition.

Well, I listen to all the great ideas from planting trees to marble statues and watched these people go from room to room in the barracks begging for votes. It occurred to me that at some point in time my life could depend on the judgement or actions of these people. That's not a comfortable thought.

The election process passes, at the expense of study time. The next natural step in the progression is the "class meeting". Where all the insignificant issues get to be decided. Here again, at the expense of study time. When I got to listen to the conversation, I realized just how important it was to have a class tee shirt and not minimize the importance of having pizza brought in to the dining hall on Wednesday nights during free-time.

The classroom experience was really cool. The class marched to class after morning formation. The instructorship was comprised of knowledgeable police officers and troopers from around the state who had completed the required classes at the academy to gain the status of instructor.

The real truth is that many of them met their demise about a mile from the campus at the local watering hole. Here's the picture; the class is seated in the classroom waiting for the instructor. The Cadre enters the room and informs the class "Sweats out front, three minutes." Translated, your instructor is either sleeping it off or is too hung-over so I'll punish you with an extra three mile run to burn up the time block until your next class.

Anyone with mild observation skills could begin to see the makeup of the Law Enforcement Community.

However, there were some great instructors that inspired with word, thought and insight. I find it a real pleasure to listen to an officer that has developed a special skill. Albeit, accident investigation, interview, narcotics or crime scene. Dedicated people are focused and can open a valuable tool box. The real trick is to learn the proper use of the tools and then develop new applications.

The last but most revealing point of this period is that you begin to learn what your classmates really are. I recall being called to formation at about eleven in the evening. We were informed that a guest instructor had observed six cadets smoking in the head. Only five stepped forward. The great fear was being booted from the academy. The sixth, the one that didn't step forward, was my roommate.

That told me something about his character. As time went on, that same officer, my roommate at the academy, lied on the stand in superior court.

If there is any one thing a cadet should take from the academy it should be an understanding of how valuable your trust is and how important it is not to misplace it with unworthy people. Professionalism, though often preached, is like true religion, seldom found.

I'm here to tell you the five guys that stepped forward, were all good career cops. All remained in the academy, receiving five gigs for their transgression.

This point should be the most important point you take from this book. The most valuable possession of any police officer is integrity.

Think of it this way. In a courtroom, you are absolutely naked. No badge, no gun, no uniform. The only thing you bring into that room is the facts of the case and your integrity. If you establish your integrity, you'll find it will be more valuable than the facts of the case. Sure, you may lose a case or two at the beginning but as time goes on, judges and attorneys will learn what you are and after a brief period your integrity will be established and the courtroom will become second nature to you.

The last segment of the academy is devoted to practical applications. Firearms, driving, crime scenes and vehicle stops. I call this the nuts and bolts time because it's where it all comes together.

My father was a Maine Guide. During my early years I learned gun safety and became rather accomplished with the use and repair of them. Firearms qualification wasn't a real problem for me. In my time at the academy thus far, I had kept a relatively low profile. However, the Cadres had done their homework and found out that I was a fair hand with firearms. Well, when push came to shove, the show was on.

It all started with the shotgun segment. The instructor started us with clay targets. Here again, I laid in the weeds. I have achieved a state championship in trap shooting. So after being introduced to an 870 pump action shotgun, we all got our turn at shooting a moving target. The gun was a typical police shotgun, cylinder bore. That means that the gun is basically a close range weapon.

Well most of the shooters had never shot a shotgun, let alone at a moving target. By the time they got the front bead on the target it was out of range.

So it was shoot and miss. There was a female cadet standing with me and she said "I'll never hit that thing." I called her off to one side and explained the situation in simple facts.

I explained that the target was flying straight away from the shooter. The easiest shot you could ask for. Then I explained that the trick was to put the bead on top of the target quickly and shoot. I told her to shoulder the gun, look for the target, bead over it and shoot. The instructor overheard me and called her to shoot next.

Well she hit the first target, the second and so on. So naturally the instructor had to call me up next. I need to explain that the trap, the launching machine, was really spent. The spring was gone so it didn't have very much power. Frankly, it couldn't pull a sick whore off a piss pot. The instructor gave me two shells without saying a word and put two targets on the plate. I could see that he was going to make an example of me.

I suggested that he move the targets as far forward on the plate as possible to give them more thrust so he did. The truth is, by moving them forward, both targets would fly together instead of spreading out. The instructor backed away from the trap and awaited my call of pull. I called pull and both targets flew close together. My first shot broke both targets and my second shot was at the biggest piece of the broken targets. I left the biggest piece as a cloud of powder, opened the shotgun, handing it to the instructor while saying "next."

I wasn't required to shoot anymore clay targets.

The second phase of firearms was the sidearm. Now it's semi-autos, but then the common sidearm was the Smith & Wesson model 66. Commonly referred to as a wheel gun or revolver. The .357 magnum was the state of the art at the time. It made semi-annual qualifications less costly as the cheaper 38 special ammo could be used by departments.

The first step was a one on one with an instructor, to check the sights with a selected single shoot at a full silhouette B27 target. We advanced to the ten yard line and once there, I was instructed to fire a shot and check my sights.

Let me point out a couple of facts here. We're standing thirty feet from the target and sighting in on a full silhouette target. That's like shooting at a barn when you're standing inside of it.

On the upper left of the silhouette target there is a small silhouette approximately five inches high that explains the scoring. Well, I'm just a farm boy from Maine but it seemed to me that the smaller the target you focus in, the clearer indication you have of proper sight adjustment. The fact was I knew qualification were coming so I had already performed this task at home and the gun was right on the money.

I fired my shot. The instructor advanced two or three steps and turned to me and said "you missed the target." My reply was " Sir, no sir, I hit the target." His reply was "there's no hole in the target." I replied "there's a hole in the target I shot at Sir." He said he didn't see a hole so I walked with him to the target and pointed out that my shot had taken the head off the scoring target on the upper left. The instructor looked at me and said, "where did you learn to shoot like that?"

Here again, I had been observing this instructor for nearly two hours. He was knowledgeable but very macho and kind of stuck on himself. So I sharpened my arrow and went to work. I asked if he was a Marine? " That's affirmative" was his reply. So I let the arrow go. "My mother taught me, she was a civilian employee for the Air Force." The look on his face was priceless and my answer was the truth.

Not only did I qualify but at the instructor's request I helped a female classmate qualify as well. The same gal that I gave the shotgun tip to.

The gal was tougher than a box of rocks but she couldn't hit a bull in the ass with a bass fiddle if she was locked in the stall with 'em.

I went out on the line with her and the instructor said he wanted to see just how I was going to correct this young lady's flaws. I started off by having her shoot six rounds at the target. The bullets weren't hitting in the same zip code as the target. So I took the weapon from her and made out like I was reloading it. I didn't, all six were the spent shells. I closed the revolver and gave it back to her, advising her that it was loaded. I told the instructor to have her fire one round and I walked off to her left and down range enough to see her eyes when she shot. She pulled the trigger, closed her eyes and flinched like a bee stung her in the ass. The revolver didn't fire and I identified her problems.

I explained that the trick of shooting was to look at the target. So much for rocket science. I explained that her goal was to maintain the proper sight picture after the revolver fired. She qualified that afternoon after a week of failure. She was a happy camper. The instructor asked me where I learned that trick. My answer was another arrow, " you really don't want to know."

Our last practical was emergency vehicle operation. Now bear in mind that for ten weeks the Cadres gave us a full ration of bullshit every day. During practicals they lighten up. Once we got to the range or driving course cadets could smoke. Well, I was a little different. I chewed Beechnut tobacco and I surely enjoyed a pinch once the bus unloaded.

Our Cadre was our vehicle operation instructor. He had been badgering me for a couple of weeks prior to the practicals about how good a chew would taste. I waited until one driver before me and I offered the Cadre a pinch in such a manner that he couldn't refuse. Then I put the bag in front of him and asked when he was going to graduate from boy scouts? It worked and he took another pinch.

When it came my turn I jumped right into the vehicle. Not giving the Cadre a chance to get out. He gave me the instructions to go though the serpentine course at 35 mph and explained that the objective was not to hit any cones.

I started out, got lined up and started into the cones at 35 mph. I immediately went to 45 mph. The vehicle sway is very noticeable at 35 mph but at 45 mph the vehicle is very near leaving four wheels. I made it through the cones and as I was turning to return to the start line the Cadre was greener than Grandma's apron. I pulled up at the start line and the Cadre got out, and talked to Ralph. He was a sick puppy. I patted him on the back and softly spoke the words, "What comes around, goes around."

The next time he spoke to me was graduation day.

Graduation was held in an area high school and the night before is called class-night. During the day before graduation all text books and academy uniforms are returned and everybody gets ready for the evening meal and tops the day off with a trip to the local watering hole.

I got up at approximately four in the morning that day. I am not a drinker. I have always subscribed to the idea that "a womans ass and a whiskey glass make a horses' ass out of men," but I must confess, I like to watch the show.

I walked out to my vehicle and brought in a half-gallon of vodka and poured it into the orange juice dispenser. Then I went back to my room and got ready to meet the day.

At the morning meal I watched the orange juice cooler. The director of the academy, the staff, Cadres all kept making trips for more orange juice. I just love to see people drinking a healthy choice. About eight in the morning everybody in the place was blistered. I waited until the dining room was empty and I ran out to my vehicle and got the other half-gallon I had, and put that in the cooler without anyone seeing me and right on schedule before the noon meal the kitchen attendant refilled the orange juice despenser.

At the noon meal the dining hall looked like a soup kitchen at a temperance hall. All my classmates who were looking forward to the watering hole, slept very peacefully most all afternoon. Some didn't make it to their rooms. The Cadres however, kept going back to the orange juice cooler. I sat in the dining hall all afternoon and laughed my ass off. Not that everybody was blistered, but at the fact that trained professional police officers were drinking the stuff and wouldn't say a word about it or take any corrective action. Again, observation is a very important tool.

Graduation went off without a hitch, just a few headaches. Look out world here I come. I'm a Cop.

Meet
The Public

Armed with all the knowledge and insight gained at the academy, I returned to my patrol zone in rural York County. The zone consisted of nine towns. Acton, Shapleigh, Newfield, Parsonsfield, Limerick, Limington, Cornish, Alfred, and Waterboro. At the outset, the task of patrolling that many towns seems overwhelming. It's a cake walk if you go about it the right way.

Early on in the law enforcement game I observed and listened to other police officers. I soon noticed that they tended to socialize with other police officers.

The mindset seemed rather bias in that these officers considered the general public as they or them. I identified the disassociation very quickly. As time progressed I began to see that these officers did rather well at traffic enforcement but didn't amount to a tinker's damn at criminal work.

It is paramount for a police officer to be social within the community. Building the lines of communication takes time. Today's buzz word is "Community Policing." Simply put; get off your ass, get out of the vehicle and talk to people. Become knowledgeable of the people and what they do. Show an interest in them and human nature takes over, they show an interest in you.

A note of caution would be to show an interest but don't get too involved until you've observed and know what you're getting into. There are some really great folks within every community.

Your first job is to identify them from the ones who are not so great.

In a large patrol zone like mine, it was impossible to be everywhere at once. So, I needed eyes and ears in those several communities that would make my job easier and allow me to be more effective with my time. I cultivated conversation and professional relationships within every community.

Here's an example of those lines. Rural delivery postmen, Central Maine meter readers, gas and heating oil delivery people, store owners, and barbers all talked to me. Virtually nothing went on in those communities that I didn't know about sooner or later.

Whenever I hear the word communication I think back to my very first day on the road as a Deputy Sheriff. I was riding with a man I had known and respected for some time. He was a good policeman who had devoted his life to law enforcement and the martial arts.

He was of French-Canadian descent. He had grown up with his parents and relatives speaking only French. He attended school in the York County City of Biddeford, a very French community. The man spoke then as now with a heavy French accent and is bilingual.

On this first day he took great pains to show me all the roads of the several communities I would be patrolling. Toward the end of the day we encountered an elderly man who pulled out onto the roadway in front of us towing a homemade trailer. The trailer was fishtailing substantially. My pard made the decision to stop the man and put the blue lights on. The man pulled over and my French pard approached the vehicle on the operator's side and asked for the operator's license and registration.

After looking at the license and registration he noticed that the license had a restriction requiring the operator to have corrective lenses. He asked the driver, " Where's your glasses?" The driver replied "I've got contacts." Again my French pard asked, "I said where's your glasses?" Again the driver said, "I've got contacts."

My French pard then replied, "I don't care who you know, where's your glasses?" I just about died laughing.

My point is that when two people communicate, half of the time we must listen to what the other person is saying. But it is not enough to hear what is being said. A good communicator listens to what the other person means.

Every year in the late spring, the Tin Can Society gathered in some remote area for the Spring Burnouts. This is described as pouring motor oil onto a paved road that is on an incline, then driving a vehicle onto the oil covered pavement and spinning the rear wheels. This creates a large volume of smoke.

The gatherings were rather large and often unruly, stopping traffic and offending the general public. Sheriff's Deputies and the State Police would join and quell the gathering with a few O.U.I. arrests and the Society would simply move to another town and everything started all over again. Basically running us around all day.

After one Burnout I knew there had to be a better way. The following spring, aware of the impending gatherings, I noticed a bunch of tires pilling up at a local garage. I stopped into the garage a few times with the family car and gathered enough from the conversations to realize that the Tin Can Society was going into the town dumps at night and stealing old tires for the upcoming burnouts. I watched the garage attendant patching a tire and observed that the patch plug material was only a quarter of an inch in diameter.

I went to the department armory and got a .45 cal Thompson and several boxes of ammo. Early the next morning I visited all the town dumps and had a little target practice on the tire piles. That Spring, there were no burnouts. The tire pile outside that garage was ten feet high. I asked the owner one day about the tires and he told me all of them had holes in them that were just too big for a plug-patch. Two more target practice sessions the following years and the Tin Can Society disbanded.

Of course, it was much to the disappointment of the blue minority because they missed the bonding time. My point here is that by listening and observing police work can be proactive not reactive.

I started keeping a file system early on, in my vehicle. Every time I made a vehicle stop, I noted every person in the vehicle. I took the time to index and cross-reference every card before the end of my shift without fail. Now I'll grant you it was a lot of work. Down the road it pays off big time because I began to put together associations.

I'd make a vehicle stop for a defect, thereby enforcing the motor vehicle law, and get the people in the vehicle engaged in conversation. I'd find out who they were without ever asking them. They didn't have a clue what I was doing and I was Officer Friendly. Now this works two ways. If they are good people I've opened a line of communication and left good community relations with them. If they were not such good people they thought, and probably so, that I was not too bright.

Either way, within a year or so I learned the fabric weave of the several towns and who to associate with whom. Not to mention the lines of communication I opened by just being approachable to the public.

One summer morning I responded to a call to meet with a farmer who had found his fence cut. When I arrived I met one mad farmer. ATV riders had cut his fence and for the second night running he had been out all night rounding up his cattle. We walked down a woods road to the edge of the pasture. This man was really upset. He said he was going to sit by his fence with a shotgun and shoot them that night if they cut his fence again.

I found an old dead tree and we sat down. I could see that the man was a really hard working, good person of moral fiber. In an attempt to make him realize what he was saying, I offered him some buckshot for his shotgun.

That made him realize what he was saying and he calmed down. I asked him if he had any lumber around his barn and he told me he was a builder and had all kinds of lumber. After a few minutes we walked back to his home and went into his shop.

Together, we took a 2X6 about six feet long and laced it with spikes. We got a hoe from the barn and returned to the place that the fence was being cut. We dug a trench, placing the 2X6 so that the spikes were pointed up and exposed about two inches out of the ground. That job done, I promised to return that evening as he had heard the ATV's go by both nights at about ten.

Our culprits came through at around nine and when I got there my farmer friend came walking down the woods road with two young boys about fifteen years old. They admitted their deeds and the parents were notified. By the way the youngsters were riding three wheel jobs and all six tires were flat.

I offered them a deal that served everyone well. The boys were to spend a week helping the farmer fence his pastures. The first no-show meant juvenile court. The boys found out what hard work fencing was and the farmer gained three new friends, two boys and a Deputy Sheriff.

That farmer was the town Fire Chief. Within a matter of a few months every fire fighter in that town became another resource for me and he also became a dear and close friend. That's communication!

I kept hearing hints that a man was trafficking cocaine. The more I heard the more I listened. Within a matter of a few weeks I started looking into it.

My first step was to talk to a resident of that town who was working for the State Police. I had known him for a few years and his father was a Game Warden. One night I met the man and I told him what I had been hearing. His response to me was " I wish I could trust you with that information but it's very sensitive." That statement pissed me off so bad that it just forged my resolve to investigate further.

I started doing ride-bys and taking down the plate numbers of every vehicle in the man's yard. I used my family vehicle and my pickup as well as the cruiser. Within a matter of a few weeks I found the key to the door. One of the vehicles in the guys yard belonged to a man who was on probation for drug convictions.

After applying a little motor vehicle enforcement, the man went to a member of the State Police Drug Enforcement Unit to offer information in exchange for consideration with the DA's office concerning the pending motor vehicle charges he was facing. That Trooper came to me as he knew from the tickets, who was providing the pressure and we worked the case.

The drug arrest was made. It was based on information I had gathered from the ride-bys, and that provided by the man I had wacked with motor vehicle violations. A half-pound of cocaine was seized, several firearms and $5000 in cash.

The Trooper that refused to give me information wasn't involved with the arrest. After the arrest, he came to me and asked why I didn't call him as it was in his town. Discretion being the better part of valor, I smiled at him and walked away. That's another form of communication.

During the summer months, I spent a lot of my days off, following brooks with a fishing pole. Sometimes I caught fish and sometimes I found marijuana fields. Basically, drug people are lazy. Plants need water and these guys are not going to expend more effort than they have to. I noted the location of the fields, and as the season went on simple drive-bys completed the picture of who was involved.

I'd let them work hard until August, just before the end of the growing season. Then I'd do the harvesting for them.

One bright and sunny day, I called together a couple dozen officers of the Sheriff's Department and State Police and we harvested two tractor trailer loads of marijuana. The word quickly spread that day and law enforcement people were coming out of the woodwork to "help" with the harvest.

The same Trooper that refused to give me information a year before, now a sergeant, came in to the command post and made the statement; " I'll be happy to help you, just give me the count and the amount after we're done."

Not an hour later two guys from the DEA showed up and said; "we'll be happy to help you out, all we need is the count and the amount when we're done today." Well, I'm not the sharpest knife in the drawer, but I could see what was going on. Both the State Police and DEA wanted to get the federal off-set money for the bust. My response to both of them was "We'll discuss that later."

The next day, after I had got a good days work out of them, I told the good Sergeant " according to the federal guidelines that I just completed and mailed this morning, along with the video tapes and case reports, the amount was substantial. I wish I could trust you with that information but it's very sensitive ."

Pay back is a bitch! I learned to communicate very well.

Although, I did what I had to do, I had a much bigger point to make and I made the point along with my Chief to the State Police Sergeant. My point was; when two cops don't talk, the bad guy wins. He got the message.

On a summer day in late July, I stopped a vehicle for speeding. The vehicle was a red Trans-Am and the operator was Asian. When I looked into the vehicle I saw a spool of bailing twine. The twine is out of place in a Trans-Am, and the operator doesn't look like a farmer. Also, first crop haying is usually in the barn by July 4th.

I asked the operator " Are you tying up your tomato plants?" He said "Yes, how did you know?" I replied, "I just finished doing mine yesterday." I then asked him, "You got big ones or cherries?" He said, "Big ones!" So I asked, "Have you tried those Northern Spy ones that everybody's talking about?" He answered, "Ya, that's what mine are."

I wished him a good day and ended the vehicle stop, he went on his way with a warning for speed. I'm sure he had a nice day because he had made mine.

A Northern Spy is an apple not a tomato. He wasn't haying, he wasn't growing tomatoes, he was growing marijuana.

Later that summer I helped him harvest his crop of Northern Spies and gave him a front row seat at the courthouse. Never did tell him the difference. He used the twine to tie up marijuana plants and it hung him.

Late in my career I took a special detail one night for O.U.I. apprehension.

My son-in-law had just started his law enforcement career with a small town department and wanted to see what it was like to patrol the vast expanses of northern York County, so he rode along with me. I had to get a motor vehicle law book as I hadn't worked the roads in years.

I explained that most of the evening would be hit or miss until after midnight. I explained that the country boys had to go to the city, get liquor'd up and dance with the city girls. I worked a few speed zones and patrolled the back roads as much as possible. I explained to my son-in-law that these back woods boys were prone to driving the back roads if they were drinking.

Not even a jack rabbit moved on the back roads that night. I decided to move down into one of the villages and poke around. Upon entering the village of West Newfield, a vehicle came toward me with a left headlight out. As the vehicle passed me, I knew it didn't have an exhaust system. I turned on the vehicle and it took off going like hell. I didn't close in on the vehicle as my life or the lives of others isn't worth an exhaust system. I just kept enough pressure on it that my blue lights would been seen and the driver couldn't take any turns off the main road.

After the vehicle passed a critical intersection I turned the blue lights off and slowed to the speed limit. My son-in-law was mystified at why I didn't chase the vehicle. I just turned off the main road and took a dirt road, found a parking spot and stopped.

My son-in-law asked what in the hell I was doing. I replied "First I'm going to drain my bladder, then we're going to sit a spell." We waited about ten minutes and my son-in-law heard a vehicle coming toward us. I cut the vehicle off with my cruiser and stopped it. The vehicle had a left headlight out and no exhaust system.

The operator was under suspension and the two passengers didn't have licenses. The operator was charged with operating after suspension, operating an uninspected motor vehicle, and operating an unsafe motor vehicle.

After we cleared the stop, my son-in-law asked me how I knew that that vehicle would come down that dirt road? I pointed out the value of knowing the roads in the town, and knowing the people. I pointed out that as they knew the police were on the main road the only route back to West Newfield was either the main road where they knew we were or the dirt road that they thought we wouldn't know about. Knowledge gained from listening years before at the lunch counter of the General Store in West Newfield.

On a summer night just a month or so after I started patrolling, I received a call to respond to the Benbow Inn in Limerick for a fight in progress. I was about five minutes away and when I got there two local chainsaw jockeys were fighting at the bar.

I didn't know that it had been standard practice to wait for a backup before going in. I signed off, grabbed my night stick, and walked right in. Sure enough two guys were going at each other. There was an empty table to my left so I brought the night stick down on the table with more than a little force. Well, I'm here to tell you, that stick hit just right and it sounded like an ot-6 went off. I got their attention real quick. The two combatants stopped and looked at me. I approached them and speaking over the jukebox I informed them that they were going for a ride with me and it was their option how they got into my cruiser, the easy way or the hard way. I had their attention by applying good communication skills.

They both headed toward me and said they'd had enough fighting. I cuffed both of them, put them in the back seat of my cruiser. Just as I seated the second one, I heard cop cars coming from all directions. State Police and Deputies arrived, jumped out and started running toward me. All were ready to go inside with me. Then I broke the news; both were under arrest and already cuffed and seated in my cruiser.

I'm hear to tell you, I may not have used my brains but I earned the respect of every officer there. It seemed that that place was considered a multiple officer call.

About two weeks later I was parked in Limerick, talking to another Deputy when we received a call to respond to the Benbow Inn. We were about a minute away. When were went in I heard the comment, "Don't screw with these guys, they're County Mounties." My communication skills had left a residual effect.

I was traveling North on Rt 11 in the town of Shapleigh. There's a long flat area just prior to North Shapleigh village. I spotted this man flying a remote control airplane. I pulled over and watch the man fly his plane and he was quite good at it. I wondered how fast that little bugger was going; when the plane started toward me I decided to put the radar gun onto the plane. I put the radar gun up and the plane darted straight into the ground.

I got out and helped the man pick up the several parts of the plane and helped him carry them back to his truck. He was very thankful. I got back into the cruiser and continued on my way.

A couple of days later, I was talking to State Police Sergeant Rene Goupil, God, rest his soul, and I told him about the model plane incident. He started laughing. After he simmered down, he told me that the radar had jammed the remote control. Stupid me, I had never given that a thought.

The following day I went over to see the man at his home. I explained to him what I had done. I offered to replace the plane and pay him for his loss. He laughed and I made a new friend. He never did let me pay him for the plane.

The next time I saw the man flying his plane was in lower Limerick on Frank Carroll's lawn. I stopped and chatted with him for a few minutes and while I was talking I saw a young fellow fishing in Pickrel Pond from the area where folks pull in to launch their boats. The young fisherman kept looking over in my direction.

In Maine, Deputy Sheriff's are empowered to enforce all the laws of the State, including hunting and fishing laws. I had a feeling that this young fellow was much too interested in what I was doing. Well, here I go. Going to get a fishing license violation. Wrong!

The young man handed me a fishing license that was all legal. It kept bothering me that he seemed so interested in me. I wished him a good day and drove off. After I had pulled out of sight of the young man I ran a check on the name. It came back real quick. He was wanted for homicide in New York. I returned and arrested the fellow without incident. After reading him his constitutional rights, the man gave me a full confession without me ever asking a question.

I learned the important lesson that things never are as they seem. A simple check for a fishing license, on a roadside, netted a murder suspect. All because I seemed friendly to him when I checked his license. Communication!

I met Marshal Mike, during my first few months of patrol. Mike was a very special person. He was a man of limited abilities. Today, I believe the term is "Learning Disabled." Mike knew everybody in the small town of Acton and everybody knew him. With the aid of Fire Chief Peter Smith, Mike built a wagon to haul around a lawn mower and rake. He traveled all around Loon Pond doing odd jobs for people.

Mike wanted so very much to be a fireman or policeman but that was out of the question. However, Chief Smith made him an honorary fireman and Mike was as proud as any man could be. Every time I saw Mike I'd make it a point to stop and talk with him. Mike would give me "police information," one professional to another.

I'm sad to say that other police officers laughed at Mike, I didn't. He'd tell me who had an expired sticker on their vehicle and where they lived. The more I listened the more I found his information to be accurate.

I responded to a call for a burglary on the west shore of Loon Pond. Sure enough, a home had been burglarized and a home safe was missing. I processed the scene, gathered evidence, and the owners stated that only the safe was missing. The owners had just arrived home from a trip. I attempted to talk with neighbors but all the other dwellings in the area were seasonal and no one was there.

On the way out of the road I thought I might check with Marshal Mike.

I found Mike on the east side of the pond walking toward Pete Smith's house. Mike walked up to the cruiser and spoke real low. "I'll see you at Pete's." I went along and in a few minutes Marshal Mike walks in to Pete's driveway and motions me to go out back of Pete's garage.

Mike proceeded to tell me that he had watched two young fellows dragging a safe out of a house on the west shore, it was the house at the end of the road.

Mike went on to say that he thought it to be about seven in the evening. He identified the two and told me that the safe was in the woods, near one of the young men's home on the east side of the pond.

Mike had followed them from the scene as they road away from the west shore house, with the safe on the back of an ATV. Mike went on to tell me that they had taken the safe back to a house on the west shore and cut it open with a torch. Mike told me that they then took the safe on the other side of the road and left it out in the woods behind some pine trees.

From Mike's directions I walked right to the safe. His account was right on the money. I knocked on the door of the house and the young man came to the door. I told him that I wanted to talk to him about a crime that had been committed and he took great pleasure in telling me where to go and how to get there. He finished his narration with "You can't do shit to me I'm a juvy."

I retrieved the safe and went back to the office. That brat was in for a real surprise. I wrote an affidavit for a warrant of arrest for my little friend. In it, I included all of his comments. The next day I presented it to the District Court Judge. The Judge read the affidavit very carefully, looked up from his desk and said he would issue a conditional arrest warrant. Well, I'm here to tell you, there isn't any such thing as a conditional arrest warrant.

The Judge said he'd set the bail at $5000 cash. Translated, Daddy couldn't offer a deed to secure his release from jail. Then the Judge told me to arrest the young man after noon on Saturday. He explained that all the area banks were closed by then and my little friend would have to remain in jail until the following Monday morning before he could be arraigned.

I went to my little friend's home as instructed by the judge. I arrested my little friend, and lead him to my cruiser over the objections of Mom and Dad.

I read my friend his rights, and he didn't say a word all the way to the County Jail.

While he underwent the standard booking procedure, I obtained an additional fingerprint card, which match prints I had obtained at the crime scene. My little friend was the real tough guy; until the holding cell door closed. Within ten seconds after that cell door went clank, you could hear him bawling for "MaMa" two miles from the jail.

The following Monday, my little friend was transported in cuffs to the District Court for arraignment. Guess who the Judge was? Juvenile cases are always closed to the public but his parents were seated in the first row of the courtroom. The Judge started by reading the charge of burglary and the entire Juvenile petition aloud. The parents started to fidget a little. Then the Judge read my affidavit aloud and looked down at my little friend and asked if my quotes were accurate and he didn't answer. The Judge then asked him if he wanted to be released to go home with his parents. My little friend found his voice and answered that he did. The Judge sternly informed him that he wasn't going to be released from custody until he rendered an apology to me for his word and actions.

I got the apology and my friend got released to his parents. He was later to be found guilty with his associate of the burglary and had to pay the victims back. He got a job and grew up real quick.

These are examples of having good communication skills with the public.

NOTHING

IS

SACRED

Although we lived within our patrol zone, the police officer's home was a respite. People didn't come to an officer's home for police services. It had to be that way or the officers wouldn't get a minute's rest.

I was riding with my Chief, Bruce Woodsome one night. We received a call for a permit for a motor vehicle to be operated to an inspection station. We arrived at the caller's home and the Chief Woodsome issued the permit. After he wrote the permit he told the caller to just drop in to my house any time if he needed a permit. This man never drove a vehicle that was fit for the road in his life. Chief Woodsome had a real laugh over violating my respite.

A couple of months later the same man pulled into my yard. He wanted a permit for his vehicle. The vehicle was a junk. I explained that I didn't have any permit forms left as I had used the last one yesterday. I directed him to Chief Woodsome's house and instructed him to blow three long blasts on the horn and Bruce would come right out and help him. I knew the Chief had the day off . I also knew he had been out until four that morning and it wasn't eight yet.

I turned on the scanner and waited. The man did what I told him. What I didn't tell him was Bruce hated people blowing the horn in his yard. Then I heard Bruce's voice on the radio calling for a Deputy to transport a prisoner to the County Jail. My phone rang shortly thereafter. I answered, "Pay back is a bitch, got any permits?"

Among the State Police and Deputies, we had a great working relationship. The same couldn't be said about our respective administrators. They had to play the numbers game for budget accountability. Troopers and Deputies worked closely together and backed each other up every day. Well, boys will be boys, and practical jokes were the name of the game.

Knowing that I am of Native American descent, I'd find a pony tied to my cruiser bumper, or beads in my paycheck envelope. Just about anything was fair game. Let there be no mistake; Chief Bruce Woodsome was behind most every prank. He was great to work with.

Late one Saturday evening I was parked at the intersection of Rt 11 and Rt 25 in Limington. A Trooper pulled up beside me. He had been on me for months about my chewing tobacco. So, he started in again. He asked me why I chewed that shit? Well, I took the opportunity to sharpen the arrow by explaining that the reason why I got so many more O.U.I. cases was because I didn't leave my zone to get coffee. I explained that one never gets thirsty while chewing and the other benefit was that you didn't get sleepy.

The guy really started to believe my bullshit line. So I laid it on thick. To my surprise, he asked to try some. It just happened that I had a tin of habanero snuff in the vehicle with me that my cousin had sent to me from Texas.

I was careful to point out that a beginner should never start out with full leaf tobacco as it would make you sick real quick. Then, suddenly, I remembered that I had a tin of starter tobacco that would just do the trick for him. I pointed out that the starter tin was better as it wasn't so addictive. The arrow was aimed.

My Trooper friend asked to try the starter stuff. I explained that it was a small tin designed to give the user two helpings. I opened it, took a knife and separated the tin's contents into two half, dumping one half into his hand. Cheerfully he stuffed it into his mouth.

The pure and simple facts were: (1), that the tin would last a man for days or a week, (2), it was hotter than putting a match to gunpowder.

It took only a few seconds for the desired effect. I saw him get out of his cruiser and he was hanging on to it for dear life. He was alternating between how hot it was and how bad he was going to kill me if he lived.

I told him I had a call and had to go, and drove off. In truth, I always met State Police Sergeant Goupil every Saturday night between midnight and 1am at the Post Office in Limerick.

I got to Limerick and there was Sergeant Goupil, parked at the Post Office as usual. I told him what I had done and he started laughing and couldn't stop. He said, park your cruiser behind the Post Office and sit with me and we'll have a chew and watch the show.

I parked my cruiser out of sight and got in with Sergeant Goupil. Approximately twenty minutes later my Trooper friend entered the lower intersection of Limerick. He asked Sergeant Goupil by radio if he had seen County 11 ? (that would be me) Sergeant Goupil answered "yes, he just headed South on Rt 5." The Trooper headed South on Rt 5 and seemed in quite a rush. After a few minutes the Trooper called Sergeant Goupil again, inquiring if he had seen County 11 go back through Limerick. Sergeant Goupil answered "yes, he just went through Limerick headed North on Rt 5."

Sure enough, the Trooper came flying through Limerick headed North on RT 5. Sergeant Goupil gave him about a minute and told the Trooper, "County 11 just came through Limerick and headed toward Limington on Rt 11."

Every time the Trooper came through town, I ducked down so that it would appear that Sergeant Goupil was seated alone in his cruiser. After a while, the good Sergeant and I were laughing so much that he couldn't talk on the radio. The Trooper finally figured out that Sergeant Goupil was in on it so he pulled up beside the Sergeant's cruiser and there I was, seated right there for the front row show.

That Trooper went on to became a Troop Commander and remains a good friend.

It was Saturday morning. I passed a vehicle on RT 224 in Sanford, Maine, with an inspection sticker that had expired a year ago. I turned and stopped the vehicle, a Mercedes. I told the female operator why I stopped her and observed that she was an attractive woman, well dressed. I asked for a license and registration.

While she was getting the requested documents she asked me if I knew, Chief so-and-so, Captain so-and-so???? She dropped every name in the Sanford Police Department. I replied yes to most every name.

I went back to my cruiser and wrote a ticket for the violation. The name dropping didn't impress me a bit. As I returned to her vehicle I leaned down to the window and asked her, "Do you know Ronnie Cole?" She said "No, does he work for Sanford P.D.?" I answered, "No, he's the District Court Judge. This ticket will introduce you to him."

My Chief used to take great pride in pulling jokes on me. Hey, they were all in good fun and I enjoy either end of a good joke. I always said, I don't get even, I get ahead, and I did.

Firearm qualification was due within a week and after being the brunt of one of the Chief's jokes, I wanted to return the favor, two fold. Being rather resourceful I went to a cattle pasture and gathered a dried cow flap. I returned home and sat down to reload some ammunition for my Chief to use for qualification.

I used three grains of Bull's Eye gun powder. This powder is really very strong so it didn't require but very little. I filled the remaining void in the shell with dried cow flap and seated the bullet. Nobody could ever tell the difference.

Qualification day came and as usual I was running the lines of shooters and giving the commands. When the Chief got ready to shoot I inspected his firearm, just like all the rest. I got up and took his revolver with me, calling for a line of shooters. He came over to me and told me he needed his revolver in order to shoot.

My purpose was to get him away from the ammunition. He fell right into the trap. "Hey Chief, I've got a box of ammo right here, you're all set." Well he dumped the shells in his pocket and he was off to the line. Prior to his arrival I had let just about everyone there know what I was doing to him.

The Chief, was a total Professional. He was a dedicated man and he demanded professionalism in public and the performance of duty. He joked when out of the public eye but knew when to be serious. I never saw a man more serious when he went on the firing line. He was all business, as it should be.

On command, the Chief fired his first cylinder full of shells. I need to explain the a dried cow flap is basically nothing but grass and water. Although it might be dry, when under pressure it turns to water. Once the cartridge is fired the dried material becomes a sticky, brown liquid and sprays from the forcing cone of the barrel.

The first volley is generally shot from a barricade. The sticky, brown liquid, sprayed out of the revolver, spattering from the barricade onto the Chief's face and hands. However, due to the time restraints he was under pressure to reload and continue firing. He reloaded his revolver and continued a second volley. The rest of the line wasn't shooting they were just standing at their positions watching but the Chief never noticed.

After the Second volley he looked back at me, his face covered with brown, and said " This ammunition smells like shit." I lost it completely and was laughing so hard I couldn't stand up. He looked down at the brown liquid dripping from his hands and asked, "Where did we buy that shit?" referring to the ammunition. That only made everybody laugh more.

To this day, Chief Bruce R. Woodsome is my dear friend. I love em' like a brother. Bruce Woodsome is an honest man and a true Professional.

How Great Thou Art

I've met as many butt-heads in uniform as I did in the public. The one thing they had in common was a big ego. Show me a target and the arrows come out. It's just my nature.

The entire southern coastal area of Maine had experienced Gypsy crimes. They were stealing from stores and homes everywhere. A couple of departments had stopped Gypsies in the area of reported thefts but hadn't found any stolen property in their vehicles. The police community was working Gypsy cases and finding nothing.

Enter the Resident Agent of the FBI, Portland Office. All departments received notice of a seminar in Portland. Hosted by the self appointed Guru of Gypsy crime, The one and only Mr. FBI. I had met the man a year or so prior to the seminar. His strongest trait was narcissus.

There was a local contractor that lived in my patrol area. The man couldn't pay his bills and always had old junk for equipment. Everybody knew the man was close to broke. While on patrol one morning I noticed two new pieces of equipment in his yard. The whole town was buzzing about it. Within a few days he had the dozer at a construction site so I visited the site that evening and got a serial number. It's a good thing that I didn't touch it, I'd have got a third degree burn. The piece was hot, stolen from a construction site near Boston.

Realizing the implications of interstate stolen property, I notified the Portland, Maine office of the FBI. I spoke with none other than Mr. FBI.

The equipment was recovered. The man was charged, and I never got so much as a thank you. Mr. FBI was the hero.

Sergeant Goupil called and asked me to join him at the Gypsy seminar, so I went. We sat through two hours of How Great Thou Art. Mr. FBI talked with some man on a speaker-phone who claimed to be the King Gypsy. Two hours and not one fact was presented that would help in the investigation or apprehension of these people.

He finally opened the gathering up to question and answer. I was in the back row, seated with Sergeant Goupil, laying in the weeds. Several questions were asked and every answer was ambiguous as a politician's statements on the campaign trail.

I raised my hand and he finally pointed at me. I said "I only have one small question to ask and it's probably too elementary to bother you with." He jumped right on my entree, " No, No, please ask your question." So I did.

" If you're so damn smart, why haven't you caught these people yet?"

The whole room of nearly 150 officers broke out in uncontrolled laughter and began leaving the seminar, class over!

I was puttering around the house and enjoying a day off when I received a call from the Jail Administrator. He held the rank of Colonel. He was insistent that I drive fifteen miles to the office to get his duty weapon and tune it. Firearm qualification was scheduled the next day.

This man was relatively new to the Sheriff's Department. He was steeped in Marine Corp tradition. So much so that a Corp flag was proudly displayed in his office for the world to see.

Out of respect, stupidity or dedication, I went into the office and met with him. He handed me his weapon and told me he wanted the action smoothed up and a lighter trigger. I inspected the weapon and thought it was really quite smooth, one cylinder point was a tad out of time.

This man made the statement that he was accustomed to perfect weaponry and would accept nothing less. He went on to say that he had achieved the highest possible scores while in the Corp. The more he talked, the more I realized he didn't have a clue about the revolver as the weapon really wasn't bad at all.

I don't have to stand in it and smell it before I recognize it. Well, here I am, sharpening the arrow again. I got him to agree to test the weapon that evening, at home prior to the next day's qualification.

I took the weapon home and put a new timing hand in it. It didn't really need it but it was going to need it down the road so I thought I'd do it and get it out of the way. While putting the revolver back together I took about three turns off the mainspring adjustment screw. This makes the trigger pull very light but weakens the hammer fall to a point that the weapon will not fire.

It is a cardinal sin to touch the mainspring tension screw.

I went back to his office and handed him the weapon. He dry-fired it and looked at me and said "Excellent, You do good work!" Anybody that knew anything about revolvers would immediately know that the weapon couldn't fire. I made a point to get a promise from him that he would call me after he tried the revolver that night.

I received a call about six that evening. The good Colonel told me he had just shot a possible target. Knowing that the weapon wouldn't fire, I knew he was full of beans, but I said nothing. Had he tried the weapon and told me the truth, I could have guided him over the phone to return the revolver to an operational state.

The next day at qualification, I watched him draw ammunition and head for the line. His weapon misfired. The Range Master, stopped the line and inspected the Colonel's revolver. The Range Master immediately said "You've been playing with the mainspring and you're not authorized to make any adjustments to this weapon." The good Colonel responded "Deputy Main tuned that weapon for me yesterday." The Range Master responded, "Don't hand me that line of shit, he's a trained armorer and he would never play with a mainspring."

Not only did the good Colonel get an ass chewing, in front of department personnel, but after the Range Master tightened the mainspring he only shot an average score. He qualified but nothing to brag about.

The Colonel walked up to me and said " I don't know what happened." I looked him straight in the eye and said, "Possible" and walked off, knowing he was a liar. The sad thing is it took a while for others to figure out the man.

I had been introduced to the subject of psychological profiling during the homicide investigation portion of the National Law Enforcement Institute.

The lecturer was a retired FBI man. Though the subject peaked my interest, the program left me with several unanswered questions about the application of the science.

After returning home I just couldn't stop thinking about it. I called several FBI offices and finally spoke with Special Agent Jim Moores. In the weeks and conversations that followed Agent Moores and I hit it off right well. He agreed to come "up to Maine" to instruct a two day seminar on the subject.

He was acquainted with the area as he had worked a case in Maine a year or so earlier.

I arranged a classroom and issued a notice by teletype. The seats were filled in two hours. The night before the class Agent Moores arrived at my office, and I extended an invitation for him to join my wife and I for dinner. We had a wonderful meal and we hit it off really well. We shared the same philosophical views on law enforcement and life. A life long friendship was forged.

After a ration of ham and eggs the next morning, we were off to the classroom. As I approached Springvale square, Agent Moores started shouting "stop the car, stop the car." I pulled over and stopped. He said " commercial artist my ass." He got out of the vehicle and approached a man who was painting the cross walk on the pavement and I heard him say to the man; "Commercial artist, you lying sack of shit." I then recognized that Agent Moores was talking to a member of the local police department.

Agent Moores got back into the car and said "there's nothing I hate worse than a liar. When I was up here working that guy told me he had a substantial second income as a commercial artist. Artist my ass."

I knew then, Special Agent Jim Moores and I were cut from the same cloth.

This guy was obviously lying to impress Agent Moores, but lies have a way of catching up to people.

During the first day of class, two State Police Detectives walked into the rear of the classroom and demanded to speak to Agent Moores. They wanted Agent Moores to profile a case they were working on. He was polite and suggested that they call his office and he'd be pleased to help them. They didn't get it. One of them became insistent that Agent Moores look at the case now as they were State Police.

I'm here to tell you that Agent Moores really showed his colors as a professional and dedicated man. He took them off to the back corner and explained that sixty people were seated, waiting on him and he was obligated to them. He suggested that they could have enrolled in the class but since they chose not to, their case would just have to wait and he wished them a good day and returned to the front of the classroom.

A few years later my friend Jim Moores drove "up to Maine" for a visit, with a female friend who was a police officer in Massachusetts. Jim and I talked on the phone a lot but didn't get to see each other very often, so our time together was special.

Our conversation was rarely about police work. It was more about our personal lives, woodwork, music and family updates. After he arrived, we decided to go to the Stone Ridge Tavern for a prime rib. It was about a half-hour travel time and his female friend went on and on; I made this stop, I arrested this guy, on and on, she just wouldn't shut up during the ride.

We arrived at the Tavern and got seated. Every time Jim and I would start to talk about something, this gal would butt in; I arrested this guy, bla, bla, bla.

She was stuck on the fact that she was a cop. Whoopee Do!

Realizing that it wasn't going to end I sharpened another arrow. After she finally ran out of wind, I looked across the table at Jim and said: "You know Jim, there's one place for a woman in law enforcement," I paused for effect, "out of it!" That little Honey never opened her trap the rest of the night and we had a great visit. (For the record, I don't really feel that way but the statement brought about the desired effect) Jim called me the next day and told me that the relationship had ended. I felt really bad until he told me he wanted to end it and I just helped it to a quicker conclusion. Within a couple of months Jim's hearing returned to normal so I guess everything worked out.

Narcissism is rather common in the law enforcement community. I just can't help myself, whenever I see somebody like that, I'm like a kid kicking a can, I just have to give them a kick. The fact is they are easy targets, fun to play with, but remember that most haven't enough substance to fill a thimble.

To them, the world is about ME.

Dream On Alice,
There Is
A Wonderland

If one is a good police officer, over time, you learn more than you want to know, especially about your brother officers. Previously I mentioned that it is important not to misplace a trust. That's easier said than done.

It's not healthy to keep everything you see inside. I am certainly blessed as I have a wonderful wife. She's much more than a wife, she's my best friend. I always had a friend to talk to. She has been my relief valve for years.

Like all new officers I started out with the belief that all police officers were moral and generally good people. I guess all may start that way, but many fall prey to transgression that make them less than honorable people.

The first day of the academy, the cadet is introduced to the "Law Enforcement Code of Ethics." I read it, learned it, and found myself using a higher standard than that code. Every day my goal was to make my wife and family proud and never bring shame home to them. I accomplished my goal but along the way I learned a lot about people that I really didn't want to know.

I was South bound on RT 11 in Shapleigh. It was mid-morning. I observed a vehicle headed North with an expired inspection sticker. I turned and stopped the vehicle.

There were two females in the vehicle. The operator was 5'6", blond with blue eyes, and 160 pounds. The passenger was 5'7", brown hair and 110 pounds. I approached the vehicle and asked the operator for a license and registration. She couldn't find the registration but handed me a license. I told her I had stopped her for the inspection sticker and went back to my cruiser.

Back then, all the licenses in Maine were paper without photos. I looked at the license and the physical description on the license matched the passenger not the operator. I called dispatch for a license and registration check but the DMV computer was down. That was common in those days.

I knew I had something more than an inspection violation but I didn't know what it was. I thought about the situation and decided to write a ticket for the inspection violation. I made the ticket out for the inspection violation in the name that was on the license. I knew the license didn't belong to the operator.

What I did know was that if the operator signed the name that was on the license, she was transforming a simple inspection sticker violation into a felony by committing forgery. I returned to the stopped vehicle and the operator cheerfully signed the ticket. Now I had a felony. All I needed was confirmation from DMV. I completed the stop and the ladies went on their way.

Within seconds after they left, I got my information from DMV. The plate registration and physical description matched the operator and it wasn't the name on the ticket. I had the felony. Within a minute or so, My Chief called me on the radio and requested that I give him a telephone call as soon as possible.

I got to a payphone within a couple of minutes and called him. He told me that he had heard the reply from DMV and asked what I had? After I gave him the details he told me he'd meet me and we'd pay the operator a visit. He told me that she was the girlfriend of a high ranking local police officer and she was knowledgeable about criminal activity in the area.

I was beside myself. This local policeman was married, had a family and a good position. What was he doing? The Chief and I met a few minutes later and we paid the lady a visit. I guess it was about a half-hour after the stop.

When the woman saw us standing at the door she lost it.

She went into a panic attack and on an on. After a while we got her calmed down. She told us that she was sorry but her license was suspended and she needed food for the baby so she drove. I explained that she had committed a felony and it was going to be referred to the DA's office.

She began to talk and nothing was sacred. She was a wealth of information.

After a very few minutes, an unmarked local cruiser pulls into the yard and Officer Romeo get out. It didn't take a rocket scientist to see the strong resemblance between him and the baby.

I completed the interview while my Chief handled Romeo. What a sleeze!

She provided really good information that solved several burglaries. She was convicted and placed on probation but, Romeo's story doesn't end here.

A year or so later, I was on patrol when I received a message to call the Chief. I called and he asked me, in his usual manner, "What are you doing tonight?" Translated that means, I've got something going and I want you to join me. I responded, as I usually did, " What time are you picking me up or am I picking you up?" He said "I'll pick you up at six." That was our entire conversation.

That evening at six sharp the Chief picked me up. He told me we were going to assist with a gambling raid. We arrived at a local P.D. and were invited to have a seat in the squad room. We waited until about eight and Officer Romeo came in the door and shouted "It's all off, go home." The Chief had a brief conversation with him and we left. The Chief dropped me off and that was that.

At ten that evening, I got a call from the Chief and he was blistering mad.

It seems that he had gotten a call from the Sheriff. The Sheriff had received a call for the local Chief. The local Chief told the Sheriff that either the Chief or I had leaked the information to the intended targets of the gambling raid. My Chief was pissed to say the least.

I know he never said a word and I know I didn't. After the Chief calmed down, we put together a plan. I placed a call to the head of security for the telephone company and requested a printout of all of local P.D.'s calls for a twenty-four hour period, while the Chief identified the targets of the raid from his contacts inside the local P.D..

I got the printout early the next morning. Using a reverse directory, we identified three calls made from a private line in Officer Romeo's office, to the homes of three of the targets. The Chief brought the Sheriff up to speed.

This was Saturday morning.

I've already mentioned the qualities of Chief Woodsome but there's something I didn't mention. One should never question his integrity. That's poking a bear with a dull stick. The Chief called me Sunday night and advised me that he was picking me up at eight in the morning and he did.

We traveled directly to the local P.D. and waited outside the local Chief's door. He arrived about quarter of nine. That allowed my Chief a little time to get more pissed off. We walked into the office and Chief Woodsome put the printout on the desk asking " Do you recognize that?" The local Chief asked, "How did you get this?" Chief Woodsome, being real tactful responded, "Just read it, especially the three calls highlighted in yellow."

The look on the man's face was priceless. He looked up from his desk speechless, as he knew he'd made a serious mistake. Chief Woodsome very calmly spoke these words; "Before you go throwing shit around you'd better clean up your own pile." On Chief Woodsome's lead we turned and left the office without another word being said.

Our Sheriff got an apology that morning. It was none other than Officer Romeo again. Romeo was a dirty cop. Sadly, his kind never go away.

The Sheriff's Department has jurisdiction throughout the County. Many investigations brought me into towns that had police departments. As a professional courtesy I would advise them if I had business in their town, and invite them as they might obtain information that could be of value to them.

That sounds good but in two communities it didn't work that way.

I was investigating a number of burglaries that had similar evidence, points of entry, items taken, foot prints, tire prints, and glove prints. A meter reader for Central Maine Power observed a vehicle and two men loading a television into the vehicle outside a seasonal dwelling. He got the registration number and reported it to me. This was the break I needed to crack the case.

I checked the registration and ran a criminal records check on the registered owner. Sure enough, this guy was on probation for theft convictions. His current address was in a community that had it's own police department. I notified that department that I would be in their town to interview the man.

I went to the address and knocked on the door. No answer at the door so I left. I did the same thing the next day. I knocked on the door and no answer. This time I asked the next door neighbor what time the man was usually home. She replied that he's usually home in the daytime but both yesterday and today he went off with the police just before I arrived.

About a hour later, I returned to the house, the man was home. I walked into the hallway and observed three televisions, several VCR's and a computer piled on the floor. My first words to his were, "I'm here for these," pointing at the pile, "and you." The first words out of him mouth were, "Hey the cops said they wouldn't rat on me if I helped them."

I invited him to help me load the stolen items into my cruiser and ride with me to the Sheriff's Office. He did and subsequent to advising him of his rights, he provided a detailed statement about several burglaries. Going by my motto, "When You've Got Em By The Balls, Their Minds and Hearts Will Soon Follow," he provided the names of everyone involved and all were arrested and later convicted.

While professional courtesy isn't really a trust, I learned a lot from that experience. Seemingly harmless information could make your work more difficult, depending on where the information goes.

Later on I learned a lot about the police officer that picked up my burglar. He made him promises. I was talking to a detective, who's desk was located next to him. This detective was pissed and when people are in that frame of mind it's easy to get them talking.

The detective had caught this other officer, going through his desk, reading information the detective had obtained through interviews, and using the information by referring to the information as coming from a confidential informant in affidavits.

That detective left police work shortly after that incident, what a terrible loss to the profession. Unfortunately, that happens a lot in the business.

A young man arrested by me for several burglaries, escaped from the transport Deputies at District Court. He returned to the lakes area and started breaking into seasonal cottages in remote areas and living in them as he knew he couldn't return home and it would only be a matter of time before he would be arrested again.

He called the County dispatch twice and asked to talk to me. Both times I was off duty. Another Deputy took the messages directly from dispatch so I never got them. Both times he called the young fellow and threatened him with arrest and so on. This had a reverse effect on the young man and only incited him to continue on with his game.

In passing one day, a dispatcher asked me if I had received the messages from the escapee. I told him I hadn't and he told me who took the messages.

This was all news to me. I called the Deputy and never said a word about the missing messages. I asked him how he was doing on the case. He told me he was right on top of everything and he expected to arrest the young fellow the next day.

The chase was a sight to see. Cottages were being burglarized, ATV's were being stolen, and it was a horror show from the start. I told the Chief what had happened. Both the Chief and I agreed that the Deputy was on his own.

He wanted the case so badly, he could have it. That Deputy ran his ass off chasing shadows.

The Chief called me after the chase had gone on for a couple of weeks and asked me to please put an end to it. I told him that I would arrest the guy but I would have to use my fellow Deputy to do it. I didn't mean the word use in the traditional sense and I explained that to the Chief. He and I were on the same page and he thought it might teach the Deputy a lesson.

Within a day, I found out where the young fellow was living. He was living with a woman who had two daughters that were his age. The woman, fearing that he would be having designs on either of the daughters, was providing him with his needs to protect them.

I used another party to tell my fellow Deputy where the young fellow was living. Predictably, he drove in the driveway and the young fellow went out the back door. Knowing the Deputy, I knew he would arrest or summons the woman, and he did.

My fellow Deputy had done exactly what the Chief and I knew he would. He had performed his role to perfection. The next morning I got a call from the woman's attorney, she wanted a deal. I called the DA's office, told them what had happened and my next step was to meet the woman in the attorney's office.

She told me that she had planned a trip for the next day to go to a movie and the young man would be with her and her two daughters. She told me the route and the time she was leaving. My only input was to make sure that the young man was in the rear seat of her vehicle as it was a small two door.

The Chief borrowed a wrecker and blocked the road on a narrow bridge and I parked my pickup truck in the woods a few hundred yards from the bridge.

The vehicle came by right on time and the young fellow was in the vehicle seated on the rear right. When the vehicle reached the bridge, it had to stop and both the Chief and I had the young fellow trapped. The arrest was made and on the way back to the county jail the young fellow asked me, "Who the hell is that Deputy I've been playing with for the last couple of weeks?"

I had a Sergeant seated with me who heard the whole conversation. The kid told me, "I didn't want to do all those breaks. I tried to call you to end it but this guy thinks he's something."

That Deputy was not in on the arrest, and he was pissed. He was even more pissed when he went to the Chief. The Chief told him which end was up real quick. It comes as no surprise that the man had a rather lack-luster career. He was a very bright man, well educated, but couldn't control his temper or his desire.

Shortly after that incident he wasn't selected for a Sergeant's position. The tragedy is he didn't know why he wasn't promoted. I attempted to help the man but he wouldn't listen.

He had doubled up with me as a new man. I showed him the roads and introduced him to people in the several communities. Giving him the leg-up that I never had. He was a very personable man and interacted well with the public.

When he asked me how I got so many criminal cases, I explained leverage to him. That is stopping a vehicle for multiple violations, realizing the operator is associated with criminals, you write every violation you find. When the person's license is hanging in the balance, that person has serious motivation to provide you with good information in exchange for a plea bargain with the DA's office.

My understudy didn't listen very well. Some months later, he had stopped a man for multiple vehicle violations. The man was a small-time marijuana dealer in the community. The Deputy didn't write any paper but was promised all kinds of information.

It was pathetic watching this Deputy running around chasing bullshit stories. He was running himself into the ground and getting nowhere. I stopped the man a month or so later, his license was suspended and I arrested him. He offered all kinds of information. My response was after you're bailed out give me a call. I wouldn't suggest you call the other Deputy cause you've given him nothing but bullshit and that doesn't cut it with me.

He got bailed and actually made a couple of controlled drug buys for me, leading to arrests and convictions. The Chief and I talked it over and I have never told the other Deputy that his "informant" had produced for me. I left him in wonderland.

As a patrol Deputy I was developing a lot of narcotics cases and convictions. So much so, that we had informally formulated a drug team. The Chief and I just selected men that would do a designated task every time. The process seemed to work, arrests were made and everybody came home alive.

Let there be no misunderstanding, drug raids are a dangerous business. You never know what is on the other side of the door. Firearms are most always involved. Generally drug raids net a seizure of firearms, drugs and large sums of money.

The team consisted of the Chief and I as full time policemen and several reserve or part time officers. Each member of the team is trusted to perform his assigned task. Trust is the operative word here. The least little mistake and somebody gets hurt or killed.

We had been on a good roll and had successfully pulled off ten or a dozen raids over a couple of months. The team was doing a good job.

Every month we had a division meeting. The patrol division would meet and new procedures were discussed, intelligence shared, and other associated business. During one particular meeting two of the patrol guys started bitching that they weren't included in the drug raids. They pissed and moaned for quite a while.

After the meeting everybody went home. I was in the office doing some catch up paper work. The Chief called me into his office and asked me if I had anything else going for drugs. I told him that I was one controlled buy away from doing another raid. He asked if we might include the two guys that were bitching about not being involved.

He and I took a ride and looked at the dealer's house. It was a small, one story, camp located in a rural area. Two windows and a door in front, and two windows in the rear. The physical layout of the property to be hit has a lot to do with officer safety. We both agreed that it was a straight-forward layout and we would use the two officers.

A couple of days later, after another buy, I obtained the search warrant and we were good to go. In Maine, all search warrants, unless specifically requested, are to be executed during daylight hours. For officer safety, the optimal time is just after sunrise. The targets are usually sleeping and officer threat is minimized.

The Chief called the two officers and directed them to meet us the next morning at an intersection a half mile from the dealer's house. One man was ten minutes late, the other pulled his cruiser too far off the road and got it stuck. The Chief gave them explicit instructions. One was to go to the front left corner of the camp. The other, would go with him through the front door. I was to go to the right rear corner. No one was to leave their assigned station until directed by the Chief. The officers were to pull up and get to their assigned positions as fast as they could run. We paired up, the Chief jumped in with me and the raid was on.

When we pulled up in from of the camp, one of the officers remained seated in his cruiser signing off on the radio, the second was putting his hat on standing outside the cruiser. I looked at the Chief and we both ran for the door. I said I'd hit the door low. I hit the door and it opened. The Chief was through as the dealer was loading a shotgun. We disarmed the man in a brief encounter and cuffed him within seconds.

The two officers walked in, completely oblivious to what had just happened. The Chief instructed the two to transport the prisoner back to the jail and wait for him to return to his office. One of the officers asked, "I thought you wanted us to help with the raid?" The Chief gave his order a second time. The order was a bit louder and not ambiguous in the least.

After they left we completed the search. We found the usual drugs, cash and firearms. After processing the evidence and completing the inventory we returned to the office.

The two officers were waiting as ordered. They were called into the Chief's office separately. I know because I head his door close twice. Both times the walls shook. Both men never asked to go on another drug raid again.

Police work, by its nature, can be dangerous. Drug raids are always dangerous. Mistakes get people hurt or killed. With no blame attached, there are some people that can perform under that kind of pressure and there are those who can't. Many of those who can't, still see themselves as completely capable of that line of duty. Knowing what hangs in the balance, officers who can function under that stress are very reluctant to tempt fate with inexperience. So some do drug raids, others dream about them. Dream on Alice, this is Wonderland.

GUM SHOE

I got settled into a closet for my office as a detective. Ya, that's a fact. My office had been a large closet. It had been the armory for the department.

I believe it was 12' by 6'. It was all I needed and to tell the truth, I didn't spend much time there anyway. I was always on the go and found more peace of mind doing reports at home.

I received a call one morning to meet with the Medical Examiner at the scene of a fatal house fire. A female Deputy was hanging around to get a few tips. She wanted to be a detective. Well, she was hanging around the office for one reason, she wanted a man. She asked to go along and I said sure. All the way to the scene she was asking questions about different people. Was this one married and so on.

I arrived at the scene and met with the Medical Examiner. The body was on a box spring in what appeared to be the bedroom of the home. It was really charred. The Medical Examiner, the Fire Marshal and I discussed the scene. The Fire Marshal had determined that the cause of the fire was a faulty heater. Foul play was ruled out and the death was accidental.

The Medical Examiner did want photographs, so I instructed the gal with me to get the camera from my vehicle. Now, the Medical Examiner was just like me. Henry Ryan had a sense of humor. He detected that my assistant was rather new and wasn't really focused on the task at hand.

Well, I thought it was about time to sharpen another arrow.

While she was gone I put in a fresh chew of beechnut. She returned with the camera and we were off to take a few photos. After I finished with the camera, I made my way to the charred body. I made a move as if I had broken off one of the charred chunks of the body and put it in my mouth. I chewed a few times and spit. I looked over at her and said; "Just right, well done."

I'm here to tell you, she blew everything she'd eaten for the last week. I thought Henry would die laughing so hard. She never asked to ride with me again and I never did tell her the truth.

Over the years that I patrolled the several communities in my zone, my card file had become rather large but comprehensive. I had one hell of a leg up on who ran with who and a pretty good idea of what they were up to. Not having to deal with the everyday zone complaints, I had a lot more time to devote to catching criminals.

It didn't take long before I was clearing cases, and transporting folks to the county jail. Along with criminal investigation, the Chief directed me to do all the internal affairs investigations.

My usual day consisted of getting to the office around six. That way I could do the day's paperwork before everybody arrived for work. I never knew what was coming through the door next. I went through my morning tasks, I'd go to dispatch and review the complaints from the previous night, and go into the jail to get the list of all prisoners. I had a wealth of criminal information right at the office, all I had to do was gather and read it.

A young Corrections officer came to my office one morning just as I arrived.

It was obvious that something was bothering him. I invited him in to the closet to talk. He was concerned that his telephone service had been disconnected. He said that he had received an overwhelming telephone bill and wasn't able to pay it. He went on to say that the majority of the calls on the bill were placed from the Sheriff's Department and were billed to his home and he gave me his home phone number. I told the youngster to bring the bill in to me and I'd look into the matter. He agreed and left the office.

That same afternoon I got information about a man that was selling marijuana in Limerick. Thus far, the guy was just a simple thief, doing burglaries. The fellow came from a good family. His folks had a farm and worked hard every day. He was lazy and not very bright.

That evening I traveled to Limerick. Sure enough, there he was, selling joints in front of the barbershop. I was driving an old beater Chevy. It was as far away from a police vehicle as you could get. I turned up my radio and leaned against the hood of the vehicle. He approached me and asked if I was new in town. (I'd arrested him twice before) I told him I was and asked him if there was any action in this one horse town.

He bit and offered me a couple of marijuana joints for five dollars each. I bought them and we continued our conversation. He asked me what I did for work and I told him I was the personnel director at the Phinney Motor Inn down in Alfred.

He asked where it was and I told him if he had the time we'd ride down and I'd show him. He said let's go, so we were off to Alfred. The catch here is C. Wesley Phinney was the Sheriff, and Alfred is the town the county jail is located in.

We arrived at the intersection of Rt 111 and Rt 4 in Alfred. I asked the man by name to open the glove box and hand me the radio mic. He opened the glove box and recognized the police radio. He looked at me and asked how I knew his name. Then it dawned on him who I was. I took the mic and notified the jail I had a prisoner and to open the security door.

That was the end of this guy's entrepreneurial endeavors.

While I was in the booking area, I observed a prisoner seated at the telephone table. He was making a call. I overheard him bill the call to his home phone and he gave the number. The number was the same home phone number that the young Corrections Officer had given me that morning. Once he had completed the connection I walked up to him and placed him under arrest for theft of services. I just happened to be in the right place at the right time.

I got a call one Sunday morning. The Chief told me that a certain Deputy was preparing a search warrant and he feared that it might be hastily done.

This was the same Deputy that had taken my messages from dispatch months before. The Chief asked me to take a ride to the office and make certain that the affidavit and warrant were correct in every detail.

I had planned to spend the day with my wife and family but I headed for the office. I knew the Deputy hadn't had much experience with search warrants. I asked him to show me what he had accomplished with the process. That man made the sorriest statement of his life. He said " You're just in here to steal my case." Well, I had to give up my day to hold his hand but I wasn't going to take a ration of bullshit while I was doing it.

I put him right up against the wall and made it real clear that I had given up a day with the family, and that the Chief had asked me to make sure the affidavit and warrant were correct to the last detail. I also told him what he could do with his case. He then asked if the Chief thought he couldn't be trusted. The truth is the Chief and I didn't trust him. He was impetuous and hotheaded. Those were the same traits that impeded his promotion to Sergeant.

After I let go of him, he got the message that I was serious. What he didn't realize was the relationship and reputation that the Department had established with the judges with regard to the accuracy and factual preparation of all our warrants. He had a pretty good grasp when I finished with him. I got his attention when I explained that one wrong statement, miss-spelled word, on either document could void his whole effort and the bad guy walks away.

He gave me the affidavit and I read it. He had articulated his probable cause very well, in fact, he had done a great job. The other portion of the affidavit and the warrant is to identify the structure to be searched, what the search is for, and directions to the location of that structure. After reading it, I suggested that we go for a ride.

The ride paid off. He had the wrong directions to the residence and had described the house next to the one he wanted to search. The Chief was right.

He had to redo the affidavit and I gave him a few pointers. The finished product was very good.

I called the Chief and told him what had happened. Here again, we both knew the man was capable, he just did things impetuously at the wrong time.

He served his warrant, searched the house, and made the arrest. In was one of the few cases he had that didn't go to trial, the man pled.

Some police officers never learn the most valuable lessons. The accuracy and comprehensiveness of a police report stands the most rigorous of examinations. When a police officer establishes a reputation for accurate and comprehensive reports, court time is diminished substantially.

Early on in my career, I received a letter from a Deputy District Attorney. The lady wanted additional information concerning a case, that wasn't in my report. I called the lady and subsequently went to her office. I closed the door and started the conversation by telling her that I never wanted to receive another letter like hers again. I asked her to tell me what made a good police report.

In the next two hours with her, I learned more about criminal investigation than any police school ever provided. That woman and I formed a friendship that has lasted for years. She is responsible for much of my success as a police officer.

Her general reputation among my fellow officers was that she was too demanding and they hated her. That told me a lot about their work. I never got another letter from her and I didn't have many trials either, mostly pleas.

Thank you Pam Lawrason, you made me a better police officer.

I received a call one night to meet with the Waterboro Fire Chief at the scene of a structure fire in South Waterboro Village. I arrived at the scene and the firefighters were busy cleaning up equipment. I located the Fire Chief and he told me that he thought the fire was an arson case.

The structure was located about three hundred feet from the Fire Station so the firefighters were at the fire scene real quick.

They had managed to extinguish the fire within minutes. The interior of the structure was really well preserved. The Fire Chief told me that he had notified the Fire Marshal's Office and one of their officers was on his way to the scene.

While I was talking to the Fire Chief and the owner of the house, the couple who were renting the house arrived. They asked what had happened and I told them that a fire had broken out in the house. Their reaction was not the usual panic over loss but where they would stay. Within minutes they left after telling me that they would be staying with the woman's mother in Buxton.

Joe Levasseur arrived from the Fire Marshal's Office. Together with the Fire Chief, we entered the house. Immediately, we identified a fire trail going down a hardwood stairway into the basement. It was obvious that the fire started at the top of the stairway and traveled down toward the basement. The trail of burn was very narrow at the top of the stairway and got wider as we traveled down the stairs.

The trail traveled over a concrete floor to a pile of clothing. Joe and I both agreed that this fire scene was the most pristine arson scene an investigator could ask for. We came out of the house and developed a plan.

Joe would do the photography and start processing the evidence at the scene, while I started the investigation interviews.

I had been working with a group called The York County Fire Chief's Association for a few months. One of the several issues we were developing with that group was to alert the firefighters to be aware of traffic while responding to a fire to avoid motor vehicle accidents. To watch closely at intersections and especially parked vehicles that might pull out without warning.

I spent the next six hours interviewing every firefighter that responded to that fire. While I was on patrol, I learned the value of the volunteer firefighters. It was these people who came out of their homes late at night to help at accident scenes, man the rescue units, direct traffic and fight fires.

They're the heart and soul of their communities.

It was past midnight when I spoke with one firefighter, who

saw a vehicle parked just a short distance from the fire scene. His description of the vehicle, described the vehicle that was being operated by the couple that were living in the house.

I asked him to take me to the location and he did. It was a dirt surface and the tire prints were very legible. I photographed the tire prints and got a signed statement from the firefighter.

I finally got back to the scene at about three or so. Joe was still gathering evidence. Processing an arson scene is a long job. Evidence has to be cataloged, packaged correctly, and ever location has to be measured and identified. I assisted Joe and we finished the scene at about eight in the morning. During the entire time the Fire Chief remained at the scene to assist in whatever way he could. Chief Kevin Theriault was a dedicated man.

Joe and I got a bite to eat and Chief Woodsome caught up to me and asked me what I had. I told him and he asked the names of the couple that lived there. I told him who they were and that I had already identified them, when they arrived at the house after the fire. I had requested dispatch to run motor vehicle and criminal checks on both but hadn't been to the office yet to read the replies.

The Chief told me he had just passed the male individual. He was driving North on Rt 202 in South Waterboro. I didn't give that fact much thought until a while later.

Joe and I arrived at the Department. We were both tired and rather spent. I went into dispatch and got my replies. Both had a couple of minor convictions but the male had a suspended operator's license. I thought it about time to have a talk with them.

We found them about noon and Joe and I talked to each separately. Both gave identical answers and were very rehearsed. I talked to them long enough to realize that the female was asserting her influence over the male and she was a very accomplished liar. Both said they were in Sanford shopping. I knew this was a lie, the firefighter saw that vehicle just up the road from the fire.

I casually worked my way close enough to the vehicle to see that the tires were similar to the photos I had taken. I made every effort to make them believe that I believed them. Before leaving I asked them to call me if they heard anything.

I had pieces, all we had to do was put them together. Fire trail, accelerant, the vehicle in the area, no obvious concern for lost property. Empty cabinets in the kitchen and no clothing in the bureaus in the bedrooms.

On the way back to the office I got an idea. I arrived at the office and went right in to see the Chief. Poor Joe, thought I had lost it. I came out of the Chief's office and told Joe that I was writing an affidavit for an arrest warrant for the male individual for operating a motor vehicle while his license was under suspension.

Joe looked at me and asked "What in hell does that have to do with an arson case?" I looked at Joe and told him "All is fair in love and war."

The first requirement in the procedure of bringing a charge for this offense is to obtain a certified letter from the Secretary of State that the operator's license is in fact suspended. That process usually takes a week. I made a few calls and got a State Police friend, who worked in the Traffic Division, to go to the Secretary of State Office, pick up the certified letter and drop it off to me on his way home.

Joe thought I was nuts. An operating after suspension charge is a traffic violation. In Joe's mind it didn't have anything to do with an arson case. Arson is a class A felony, the most serious classification of crime in the criminal statutes. Operating after suspension was a frequent motor vehicle violation that police officers deal with on a daily basis.

Curiosity finally got the best of Joe. He waited until I had finished the affidavit and asked me to explain what in hell I was doing. I told him I was going to arrest the man and I needed a warrant to do it. I told him that once away from his girlfriend he would be out of her control and we'd get more information if we played our cards right.

Late that afternoon the certified letter arrived. Joe and I had a visit with a Complaint Justice and I got my warrant of arrest. We started for Buxton and we both decided we needed something to eat. We were going on twenty something hours without rest or food. I pulled into a small convenience store in Waterboro. A lady came out of the store just as I was driving in and nearly stepped in front of the vehicle.

She was obviously shaken and I got out and consoled her. I told her my name was Joe Levasseur and worked for the Fire Marshal's office. She was thankful that I had been so caring of her, thanked me and I helped her to her vehicle. Joe asked me, "What did you say to that lady?" I told Joe, "I told her I was Joe Levasseur of the Fire Marshal's Office." Joe and I were so tired we both just stood there laughing as he was calling me every name in the book.

I told Joe that after we made the arrest we wouldn't say a word to the man all the way back to the county jail. The plan was that I would advise the man of his constitutional rights, and then tell him that we had no questions for him at that time. The remainder of the trip, Joe and I would have a conversation about Class "A" felonies and prison time in the state prison.

I made the arrest. I showed the man the warrant, holding my hand over the charged violation. All he could see was the bold print WARRANT OF ARREST. The man was cuffed and seated in the rear seat of the cruiser. I advised him of his rights and we were off to jail.

Joe and I had a grand conversation on the trip to jail. I honestly think we could have scared Hitler on that ride. Twice the man tried to say something and I advised him not to say a word.

As we entered the jail complex I turned, looked at the man, and asked if he still wanted to talk to us. He said yes. I went into the jail first and told the booking Sergeant that I did not want the prisoner to know what the charge on the warrant was.

The man was brought into the jail and the booking Sergeant played his part to the letter. He managed to make a point of saying that the man must be in real trouble if I had arrested him. The Sergeant placed the man in a holding cell briefly, while Joe and I went to open an interview room. The Sergeant then brought the man in to the interview room.

I advised the man of his constitutional rights very carefully and had him sign the bottom of the card and read his rights. He signed the card and sat there while I was getting a pad of paper.

I then asked him his name and date of birth. I told him again that we were police officers and that we were investigating a crime of arson. He responded, "I know, I did it. I started the fire." I looked over at Joe and Joe almost fell out of his chair. The man agreed to give us a voluntary statement. He completed the statement, implicating his girlfriend equally as himself.

After he had completed the statement, I took him back out to the booking desk and completed a summons charging the offense of arson. The man seemed rather relieved that he had confessed. His mood changed rather soon when he found out that the warrant was for operating a motor vehicle while his license was under suspension. I think it safe to say he was rather pissed.

I arranged with the Sergeant to take an hour or so to process the man. Allowing us time to return to Buxton and arrest the female. The Sergeant agreed and Joe and I returned to Buxton to make the final arrest in the case.

We arrested the female, advised her of her rights and returned with her to the jail. The case was closed.

The reason given by the man for the arson was that they couldn't pay the rent and his girlfriend told him fire victims are always given a new start by the Red Cross and the Salvation Army.

Not everything went smoothly. I made my share of stupid mistakes. Probably, the best was my class in photography 101. Every time I think of it I just laugh at myself.

I received a call one morning from one of our Deputies. He had recovered a stolen vehicle. He was requesting that I assist him in processing the vehicle for evidence. I had been using a one-step Polaroid camera but it had seen it's better days. I told the Chief that I was going to assist the man and he gave me a new 35mm camera. I asked him if it was ready to use and he said it was. I'd never used a 35mm camera in my life.

I got to the scene and started dusting the vehicle for prints. I developed several really good fingerprints. The standard procedure is to photograph the prints prior to lifting them with tape. I took three photos of each print and I was really cooking with this new camera. The adjustable focus was really great. I zoomed right in and they looked really clear in the camera.

After I had photographed all the prints, I taped and lifted them making careful note of location. I finished my work and the vehicle was towed away.

I went back to the office and asked the Chief how to remove the film from the camera. He replied, "That's easy just wind the film like this, and then press this button." He opened the camera and there wasn't any film in it. We both laughed so hard we were crying. It's good thing that I got super lifts because there weren't any photos.

To this day, I hate cameras. The saying; "Take a picture, it lasts longer," doesn't apply to me.

A mother called me one afternoon, very concerned about her son. The lad was ten years old. Mom had found several items in her son's room that had been stolen from the neighborhood. I asked her if she would bring the boy in to the office. She agreed and I told her I'd have a chat with him.

I reviewed the complaints in dispatch and found three burglaries in that neighborhood in the past couple of weeks. Two of the police reports were completed so I had something to work with in the interview.

Mom arrived with the boy. I talked with Mom first while the boy was seated outside my office. Mom said that she knew her son was not telling the truth but no matter what she did or said, she couldn't get him to explain the items in his room.

In further conversation I learned that the boy was keeping company with area high school kids. He wasn't spending any time with his friends that were his own age. He had abandoned them for the older kids.

I invited the boy in to my office. Our relationship started off with a bang. This ten–year-old boy said to me, "You ain't got jack shit on me." It was obvious that he'd been influenced by someone and was expecting a confrontation. So, the arrows got sharpened real quick.

I looked at the boy and said, "I understand you're not telling your mother the truth." He responded, "Ya, well prove I'm not. I don't care what you do, I'll take a lie detector test." I responded, "I can set it up, just sign this form." The form was for a release of medical records, but he didn't read it he just played tough guy and printed his name on the paper. Then I asked him to wait outside my office while I got his mother's signature on the form.

After he left the office I told his Mom what my plan was and she agreed.

I took a cassette recorded out of my desk and recorded four answers on the cassette. True, True Lie, and Lie. I detached the microphone and put a flat, glass paperweight on top of the recorder. Then had him come back into the room and have a seat.

I asked him to roll up his left sleeve and he did. I went through an elaborate act to attach the microphone to his arm with rubber bands. After being seated behind my desk I asked him if he was ready to start. He said he was.

I explained to him that I would ask him a question and after he answered, the polygraph, inter-personal-communication device would activate after measuring his heart beat, pulse and blood pressure to indicate a true or false statement. I instructed him to place his hand on the glass and I could see this kid was scared as hell. So we began.

"Is your correct name X. X. X.?" He answered "Yes." I waited several seconds and hit the pause button and he heard TRUE. I hit the pause button.

"Are you ten years old?" He answered "Yes". I waited a few seconds and hit the pause button again and he heard TRUE. I hit the pause button and then pulled out the police reports of the two burglaries and after studying them for a minute or two I asked, "Did you steal the Saga game set from Mrs. Z's house?" He answered "No." I immediately pressed the pause button and he heard the word LIE. My little friend lost it right there. His career as a tough-guy was over. He confessed his role in all the burglaries and named his high school friends. It seemed that the older boys planned the whole thing and sold most of the stolen items at school.

I had a long talk with the boy and made a new friend. I made it a point to stop by and visit whenever I had a minute over the next several years. The kid turned out to be a good citizen, soldier and now husband and father.

TOOLS
OF THE
TRADE

Not unlike the carpenter trade, police work requires a certain degree of natural skills. I just can't put enough emphasis on observation skills. It's like an extra sense, being aware of what is going on around you. Sometimes it's what you don't see that is important.

About eight o'clock one evening I received a call for a structure fire that was a suspected arson. I arrived at the scene and met with the Fire Chief. The structure was a ranch style home with a basement apartment. The Chief told me that the fire was contained in the bedroom of the basement apartment.

Upon entering the apartment I observed a single rose on the kitchen table. This is usually a gustier of affection. After photographing the entrance area, I advanced into the apartment and arrived in the bedroom. The fire had been concentrated on the right side of a king-size double bed.

Looking about the room there were several adult toys. I photographed the scene and left. In addition to taking photographs, I made it a practice to take along a notepad. After every photo I would note everything I saw that would be in the photo, a kind of check list.

There are several reasons for both photos and notes:
  A. Geographic layout
  B. Provide an accurate record of scene
  C. Relationship of item placement
  D. Items missing
  E. Record of event

After I had photographed the interior of the apartment, the next step is to photograph the exterior of the structure, especially the windows and doors.

I met with the resident of the apartment, a single woman approximately 30 years old. Within the first minute of conversation she was casting blame toward her ex-boyfriend. Thought not always accurate, it is important to listen when blame is cast. The underlying reason is that it provides a window into the relationship of people and may give direction to the investigation.

It is important to make a special note that blame can also be falsely cast. The objective is not to let the cast of blame have a tunnel effect on the investigation.

The woman told me that she and her boyfriend had separated. They had been apart for two weeks. She went on to say that she had been living in the apartment alone during that period and her ex-boyfriend had been calling her and wanting to get back together. She related their history as an off and on relationship marred with arguments.

I later spoke with the couple that owned and lived in the main portion of the home. They told me that the woman had separated from her ex-boyfriend. They also told me that she was not the "sister of mercy" that she wanted me to believe. It seems she had been entertaining other male friends during that two week period on a regular basis. They also told me that she was a good housekeeper and kept the apartment spotless.

After the interviews had concluded, I invited the woman to walk though the apartment with me. My instructions were quite simple. She was to walk with me, touch nothing, and identify anything that was missing or out of place.

The first thing she noted was the single rose on the kitchen table. She stated that the rose wasn't there when she left and didn't know where it came from.

The rose was about a foot in from the edge of the round table, not located near the center.

After finding several items missing from the toy collection in the bedroom, nothing else was discovered in the apartment that was noteworthy.

I did learn that the toys were kept in one draw of a bureau and not strewn about as they now were. She was upset that the apartment was in such a state of clutter. She said she kept the apartment clean all the time.

Observation of the interior of the apartment's kitchen and living room area showed symmetry, a common trait in most women homemakers. The rose not being in the center of the table and that she didn't put the rose there became important.

She stated that she had not given out any keys to her apartment and that she had changed the lock after she split from her ex-boyfriend. That became another important piece of the puzzle.

She did not notice, nor did I point out to her, that a kitchen window was unlocked. When I asked her about the window, she couldn't remember if she had opened the window or not. There was no screen on the window and it was logically the only point of entry.

My points of concern were the window and the kitchen table. I processed the vase that the rose was in and obtained several quality fingerprints. Collected a Winston cigarette butt from the ashtray on the kitchen table, and fibers from the window ledge of the kitchen window. The owner had painted the exterior trim that morning.

I called the woman to find out if she smoked and she stated that she smoked Marlboro Light cigarettes.

It didn't take long to locate the ex-boyfriend, he had been arrested for other transgressions while I was processing the scene of the fire by another department. I stopped at a local store and bought a pack of Marlboro Light cigarettes before paying the ex-boyfriend a visit at the jail.

I introduced myself to him and in passing, offered him a cigarette. I offered him a Marlboro and he stated that he smoked Winstons but at that point anything would do.

Without my asking anything about the fire incident, the man said, "I know why you're here." So I told him, "Yes, I'm here to get your fingerprint card, I got some really good prints tonight." He replied, "So that doesn't prove anything." I responded, " I hope they have some spare pants around here because I'm taking the ones you're wearing." Now the guy's starting to get the drift, he answers, "You can't prove I was anywhere near that fire." I said, "Who said anything about a fire? All I want is your fingerprints and your pants. The prints and the paint on your pants will put you at the scene."

I got a conviction for class "A" arson.

The tool that I applied in this case was simply observing the crime scene and knowing what was out of balance. A profile application would have been classic.

I have found a lot of lost hunters, lost campers, mentally handicapped folks who wondered off into the woods and criminals who fled into the woods. My best tool was observation. The trick is to recognize what is out of place and why.

A diabetic camper walked away from a campsite and got lost. I responded to the scene and after talking to his friends and observing the area, I found him within thirty minutes.

There are some facts that you need to start out with. First and most important, a man in the woods is like a goose in a barnyard. You'd better watch where you step, you might be covering something. Humans leave a trail that is as clear as day if you know what to look for.

Crushed and bent vegetation is the first key. The direction of the bend gives you the direction of travel.

Rocky surface, no problem. Small pebble craters clearly indicated a human has passed. The pebble's location from the crater, indicates the direction of travel. The moisture line in the pebble will give you an idea of time lapse.

I've omitted the easy things like footprints on the sides of puddles, and in sand, even a city cop might see that.

My point here is that an observant person can obtain a lot of information from just looking around. LOOK before you WALK. Once you've contaminated evidence, it's GONE FOREVER.

I overheard a call to a Patrol Deputy to respond to a domestic dispute complaint. Knowing that this type of call consistently proves the most dangerous to police officers, and realizing I wasn't very far away, I responded to the call. The Patrol Deputy arrived at the call about three minutes before I did.

When I arrived at the scene, the Patrol Deputy was seating a handcuffed man in his cruiser. I asked the Deputy what he had and he responded that it was a simple domestic. I walked into the residence and observed a woman standing in the kitchen area.

Seeing no threat of weapons, I did a quick visual survey of the interior of the home. I observed what appeared to be the handle of the black cast iron frying pan sticking out of the living room wall just above a sofa. Seeing an indentation to the right of the handle, I looked behind the sofa and there, on the floor was a wood handled carving knife. I observed the rest of the kitchen knife set with similar handles.

The woman did not appear to have any injuries and when asked she stated that her husband didn't harm her. She made the statement, "He got what he deserves."

Hearing the sounds of two children crying, I went into the bedroom to talk with them. I learned from both children that Dad was late getting home from work. Mom got mad and threw stuff at Dad when he came in the house.

As the two children were telling me what had happened, the Patrol Deputy had come in and overheard the children's account of the events. He realized he had arrested the wrong person.

I left the residence with the Patrol Deputy right on my heels. Once outside, he asked me, "How do you un-arrest somebody?" It was clear to me that he didn't take the time to look at the scene. He simply jumped to a conclusion and arrested the wrong person.

The man was not a threat. Officer safety is a concern on every domestic, however, it doesn't negate the application of common sense. The fact is the Deputy didn't use observation and could have caused him and the Department serious legal problems.

Once the woman was arrested, her husband UN-ARRESTED, and order restored, I left. How that Deputy bullshitted his way out of a false arrest I don't know.

I cite this incident to point out that there is no excuse for not using the tool of observation. I realize that the complaint was received near the end of the Patrol Deputy's shift. That fact does not justify a disregard for the application of basic tools.

I was called into the Sheriff's office one day to meet with the Sheriff. He assigned an internal case to me, which involved a high-ranking member of the Department. The essence of the case was that the officer was submitting expenses on a regular basis for working at the office on off-hours. The Sheriff had reason to believe that the claims were not legitimate.

I had observed this officer on several occasions, walking to his vehicle with department issue items. I knew a little about the man. Except that he had ordered me in on a day-off to repair his weapon a few months before.

I gathered reams of evidence during a two-week period. The evidence proved beyond a reasonable doubt that the claims were not legitimate. One interesting fact of the investigation revealed that on a time and date the man claimed to be working, he had been stopped, by another department and issued a warning for a motor vehicle incident. His secretary was with him in the vehicle.

Subsequent to the investigation the officer was suspended from duty. I was assigned the task of going to the officer's home and retrieving all of the uniforms, badges and all the department property the officer had.

This presented a problem because the officer was a staff person with unlimited access to all department property. Another Staff officer was assigned to join me. I was perplexed for a few minutes about the task. I knew what I had observed over the past months but I had no way of knowing what property the officer had. I told the Sheriff and the District Attorney that I had a plan.

We arrived at the officer's home and both of us displayed empathy toward the officer. The officer suggested that I start an itemized list of the department property that he was surrendering to us. I told the officer that I was so saddened by the affair that I wouldn't know where to start.

Taking command of the situation, the officer started itemizing in detail everything he was returning. He completed the list and appearing reluctant, I asked if he was sure that all the department property he had was included on that list. The officer gave the answer I was looking for: "Absolutely!"

Several weeks later, the suspended officer was charged with impersonating a police officer and displaying a badge. That investigation was completed by another agency.

Several months later that case went to trial. The list of surrendered department property became paramount at that trial. I was called to testify as a rebuttal witness. The officer had made an issue of how stupid I was that I couldn't do a simple inventory list.

I testified that because the office had a staff position within the Sheriff's Department, he had free access to all department property. I had no way of knowing what the officer had. Only the officer knew what he had and he completed the list. Therefore, only the officer would know if he failed to surrender all department property in his possession.

The officer was found guilty and a subsequent dismissal from the Sheriff's Department was upheld.

The observations I made from day to day, though casual, became important in this case. Observations are more than visual, they form what is called a GUT FEELING.

The gut feeling is another important tool. My hero in life was a Trooper. He befriended me at a young age and kept me on the right road. There is only a few years difference in age. The man said many things to me in my younger years that registered with me as I got older. I gave a lot of thought to that advice. One thing stood out in my mind that echoes today, like it did forty years ago. He said, "I've got a gut feeling that someday you'll be a good officer."

Throughout my career, I've tried to live up to that statement. I thank you Bernard Emery for giving me courage and having faith in me.

GUT FEELING to me is best defined as having enough life experience to equip a person with internal judgement skills. It's not taught at any police school, but there is a simple formula for it. Wisdom gained from life's experiences.

I was investigating a child abuse case. The victim was an eight year old boy who had been sexually abused by his mother and two aunts. The boy was removed from the home and placed in foster care.

I had met with the boy several times. It was accepted that the boy had a speech impediment. So much so, that it was difficult to discern but few words in his speech. Something kept telling me to keep meeting with the boy because, though he wasn't able to communicate with me verbally, he drew pictures that answered my questions.

I had recorded several interviews, returned to the office and reviewed the tapes. Each time becoming more frustrated that I wasn't making progress.

His lack of speech was a severe obsticle as he could not testify. I had a gut feeling that this boy was telling me something but I wasn't hearing it.

One morning, alone in my office, I decided to listen to the tapes again. At first it was the same gibberish. Then the batteries started to ware down. As the speed of the tape slowed down, the boy's speech became clearer and his response to my questions was right on the money.

I called a pediatric specialist and she referred me to a forensic pediatric clinic. The tapes were slowed in speed and every question I asked was answered in detail by the boy. The short explanation is that the boy was so bottled up with frustration, he rushed to speak.

The last interview tape was very revealing. The boy drew two pictures. When he drew second picture, he looked at his foster mother. In the tape he told me she was doing the same thing with him that his mother and aunts did. My gut feeling was right about the boy.

The mother, both aunts, and the foster mother were all convicted of sexually abusing that child. I'm sorry that it took me so long, I was stumped. But that gut feeling told me to keep trying.

I received a call one morning from a Department of Human Services Child Protective worker. I knew most of the DHS people in York County but this was a new one. She advised me that she was bringing a fifteen year old female victim of sexual abuse to my office and that she would supervise the interview.

She arrived with the young lady and immediately started telling me what she was going to require. I invited her to have a seat in my office. She continued to tell me what she expected. I listened until she was done giving directives.

I then asked, "Are you finished now?" Her reply was, " The sooner we get started the better."

Now that I could finally speak, I asked her, This is your first case isn't it?" She retorted, "Well I have my degree and I've been with DHS a while." I could see that tact wasn't going to cut it so I decided it was time to bring this lady into the real world. I asked her why she had called me and she said, "The DHS people in the Biddeford office told me to call you." I asked, "Why do you think they directed you to me?" She said, "They said you've had a lot of experience with these cases." I asked, "Did they tell you anything about the disposition of past cases?" She Said, "Yes, you get the guys and send them to jail."

Then I dropped the bomb. "Yes I do, and I couldn't give a hoot in hell about how you want things done. This is a criminal investigation, I'll conduct it, and do all the necessary steps to bring the case to conclusion. You are welcome to sit in on the interview with this young lady BUT, the first time you ask a question or say anything, you'll be doing the rest of the case alone.

Do I make myself clear?" I left the office to get the young lady and escorted her back into my office. I told the worker to make notes of any questions she might have, hand them to me, and I'd ask them.

I did a detailed interview with the young lady. Although I took notes, I also taped the interview. The young lady gave me several details, all were noted and recorded. After the initial interview, which took the better part of an hour, I invited the young lady to take a break, get a soda and relax for a few minutes. The worker had no questions and didn't take notes.

Then I asked the victim to provide me with a written statement of what she had told me. I seated her in a quiet room and provided her with statement forms and a pen. She completed the statement within an hour or so. It was near noon so I suggested that they go to lunch and then return to my office. I cautioned The DHS worker not to discuss the details of the case with the young lady over lunch and reminded her of my earlier statement.

The investigating officer is the one who testifies before the Grand Jury and in Court. If someone other than the investigating officer asked questions during the interview process, they are subject to testify. That puts them in a foreign setting, creates stress and usually complicates the case during the trial. All this is avoided by having the DHS worker remain quite.

After they left my office I read the young lady's statement. Certain details she gave in the statement didn't match the details she had given me in the interview. This is very unusual. The details were miles apart and I'm now left with serious questions about the case.

They returned after lunch and I decided to do a second interview. In my notes I always wrote the questions that I asked. I took careful pains to ask the same questions again though not in the same sequence. The end result was two interviews about the same incident, two answers, neither of which agreed with the written statement she had given to me. In short, I had a gut feeling that the young lady was lying.

I concluded the interview and escorted the young lady back out to the lobby.

When I returned to my office the worker asked, "Are you going to arrest the Step Dad now?" I answered "No I'm not." The woman went ballistic. She went into a rage and after she finally stopped to breathe, I told her that the young lady was not truthful. The woman threatened me with everything but the gas chamber and finally left.

One day a couple of months later, the Chief in passing, asked me about the status of that case. I told him the girl was lying and I didn't believe her because her accounts of the incident were not consistent. He said nothing more.

About four months later, I got a call from the young lady. She told me she was sorry and that she had lied. I got a statement from her that she lied. Her reason was that her step-dad wouldn't allow her to go out on a date until she was sixteen. She called me on her sixteenth birthday.

When I got back to the office I completed the report and added a juvenile charge of making a false report. I filed it and thought nothing else about it.

The following day the Chief came into my office with the report. He showed me letters and copies of letters that the DHS worker had written to the Sheriff, Commissioner of the Department of Human Services and the Commissioner of Public Safety. All, demanding my removal for failure to perform my duty. These letters were dated throughout the period of time that had passed since the initial interview.

The Chief, armed with the complete report, responded to all of the worker's writings. She lost her job.

I had a gut feeling and I was right. Some lame-brain liberal from a social welfare department at a college, tells these soon-to-be social workers that children don't lie. WRONG!

Another important tool is tenacity. A good cop understands that it takes time to put together all the pieces of a puzzle. Bernard Emery once told me, "Someday the light will come on." If a cop wants to see the light, he'd better be willing to work hard to find the switch.

I was dispatched to a call one morning in Limington. The only information provided to me was that there had been a shooting. I was no more than five minutes away from that location.

When I arrived at the mobile home, a woman came to the door

holding a revolver in her had. She was shouting, "I did it, I shot that son-of-a-bitch."

I took the revolver away from her and locked it in my cruiser and returned to the mobile home. The woman was hysterical. After several attempts to calm her down, I was able to learn that she had shot her husband twice with the revolver. The husband had managed to get out of the home and hitch a ride with a friend who was parked outside.

I received another message from dispatch that a doctor's office in Standish reported the arrival of a gunshot victim. The victim had two wounds, leg and abdomen.

The woman told me that she was in the kitchen when her husband arrived home after being out all night. She had found out that he was with another woman. She shot at him twice as he was leaving the living room running for the door.

A Trooper arrived and agreed to take a statement from the woman. We got her to leave the mobile home and she was seated in the Trooper's cruiser.

I brought the Trooper up to speed with the history of the event.

I returned to the mobile home and contacted the doctor's office. The doctor told me that the male victim had two wounds. One bullet was lodged in an ankle and the victim's abdomen showed an entry and exit wound. The doctor stated that neither was life threatening, he had treated the victim and had him transported to Maine Medical Center for further treatment.

I had learned that both shots were fired from inside the mobile home. One bullet was accounted for as it was lodged in his ankle. However, the second bullet had to be inside the mobile home as there was an exit wound.

The path of the first bullet was obvious as it went through the kitchen table before hitting the victim in the ankle. The second bullet remained to be found.

As I began to photograph the interior of the mobile home, two State Police Detectives came into the mobile home. After a brief conversation, one of them started telling me what I had, what I needed to do, and how they would take the case. Well, I might be just an old farm boy but I don't have to step in it and smell it, before I recognize it.

This kind of thing happens in police work. I call it the Divine Savior Syndrome. This is defined as, the world is about ME and I am God. The truth is, their bullshit didn't cut it with me and I invited them to leave the crime scene with absolutely no ambiguity in my voice.

In later years, State Police Sergeant Rene Goupil and I were seated in my shop one morning and Rene told me that he had met a terminal Frenchman yesterday. I asked him to explain.

Rene told me that he had grown up in Saco, Maine. The Saco / Biddeford area is a predominantly French community. French Canadians had relocated to the area to work in the shoe and textile mills. He told me that being called a dumb Frenchman for so many years, motivated him to earn his master's degree in education. I can tell you Rene was far from being dumb, in fact, he was one of the smartest men I ever knew.

He told me that he had to call a man into his office, the day before, and broke the news to him that he would never live long enough to be promoted to sergeant within the ranks of The Maine State Police. He went on to say that the man had taken the sergeant's examination "several times" (exact number omitted) and had never achieved a passing grade. The man was one of the Divine Savior Syndrome duo that I had met at the crime scene. Why wasn't I surprised?

I completed photographing the interior, and began searching for the remaining bullet. I searched for three hours, going over every inch of the interior. I couldn't fine a trace of that bullet.

The woman had given a statement and the Trooper transported her to jail. Not finding the second bullet, my next option was to interview the victim. I met with the man at Maine Medical Center in Portland. He told me essentially the same thing I had learned from his wife.

After the interview I informed the man that I would need his clothing as evidence. As I looked at the clothing I saw two holes in his shirt which indicated an entry and exit. When I got to the pants, there was only one hole and from his account, it had to be an exit hole. Further examination of the leather belt provided the important missing link. The leather belt had a substantial dimple, emitting from the inside. The bullet had entered just above the belt and exited at the belt line, becoming lodged in the belt.

The man told me that his clothes had been removed at the doctor's office in Standish earlier.

After several calls I visited the doctor's office. It was about eleven in the evening by the time I arrived. The cleaning lady met me and I searched the treatment room. She told me that she had cleaned the room earlier, vacuumed and washed the floors. Examination of the contents of the vacuum cleaner bag revealed the missing bullet. The last piece of evidence was located.

I received the initial call at about nine-thirty that morning. I finally located the second bullet at eleven that evening. It was worth the effort. The bullet lodged in the victims ankle was fragmented. However, the second bullet was ballisticly matched to the revolver I had taken from the woman's hands.

That is tenacity! By way of a side note, the woman's defense was an accidental discharge. The revolver was a single action firearm, which means the revolver had to be physically cocked before it would fire. Twice???

She was found guilty and went to the big house.

There is a saying in police work, EVERY DOG HAS HIS DAY. If a policeman has tenacity his day will come, it's just a matter of time.

The most needed and least applied tool, tenacity is seldom mentioned in how to police books. I have stayed away from the everyday, do it this way books, that I've read over the years. I'm of the opinion that if an officer has to read those books, he's in the wrong line of work.

My approach to investigative work has always been very simple. I just applied a few simple rules.

The first rule is that there is no such thing as a coincidence in criminal investigation. The difference between a good officer and a bad one is the good one will find the reason behind that which appears coincidental.

Look beyond the obvious and the pieces of the puzzle will go together much faster. Insight comes from knowing the people you serve.

Examples are everywhere in the business. Old registration plates on a new vehicle. Observing a known thief traveling through an area where burglaries have been reported. People without jobs spending a lot of money at the local stores.

The time element is a policeman's real enemy. Over time, so much information is processed that no one can remember everything they see and hear. I always kept a notebook in my pocket, even when I was off duty. When I overhead something in a store, barbershop, or on the street, I'd get out of sight and write it down. Though many times the statements didn't mean much at the time, a week or two later, I'd be called to a complaint and something I overheard weeks before would solve the case. I went to the notebook, found the information, and I had direction in the case.

Strike while the iron is hot. People tend to forget very quickly. Doing a neighborhood canvas two weeks after a burglary seldom nets any information. It should be done within hours of the report. Just as soon as a time frame is established.

My second rule is to thoroughly process a crime scene. Too many crime scenes end up like a police convention. Having a social hour at a crime scene is not good police work.

The scene of a burglary is not the interior of the building alone. Evidence starts with point of entry to the property, not the building. I can't tell you how many times I've seen two or more cruisers parked in the dirt driveway of a burglary scene. Thus destroying tire prints and footprints. The objective of processing the crime scene is to collect evidence, not destroy it.

Every scene has evidence. The good investigator finds it. It can be as simple as the method of entry, or the use of a pillowcase to carry stolen items. Tool marks used to gain entry, time of day, point of exit, or items taken. People are creatures of habit. Properly processing a crime scene can reveal related crimes from similarities.

I was on the road one day and observed a young man lugging a VCR while walking down the roadside in Limerick. I should point out that this young man never worked a day in his life.

I stopped and talked to him. We chatted about video movies and in our conversation he told me the VCR came from another young man who was living at an address just down the road. The second young man was equally motivated not to work. However, I knew the second young man was a thief who always went into a house through one pane of a cellar window.

I went back to the office and reviewed the patrol reports and found several burglaries in a community not far from where I had talked to the young man with the VCR. Several of the burglaries had VCR's missing. A few of the reports noted a broken cellar window pane.

The next day I was in the area and decided to stop at the address I had gotten from my young friend the day before. It was mid-winter and snowing hard. I knocked on the door and heard "Come in it's not locked." I walked through the door and there were several TV's, VCR's and other household appliances piled in the kitchen. Knowing I had nothing but a gut feeling, I looked at the young man and said, I've come to pick up this stolen property and I'd sure appreciate it if you'd help me load it. The young man agreed to help me. I had to call the Chief and get a truck because I couldn't load that much into a cruiser.

After the arrest, the young man agreed to show me each house he had burglarized. Sixteen burglaries were solved. All entries were made in his usual manner, through a cellar window pane. People are creatures of habit.

The third tool is a very simple rule. Never attack a person's dignity. I've arrested a lot of people in my career, and the majority of the time I made people feel that I got little enjoyment arresting folks. When an officer isn't verbally confrontational, demeaning, or flat out rude, people in that predicament are more likely to be cooperative and provide information that could be meaningful.

It goes without saying that if a man is in the law enforcement business any length of time, he'll be arresting the same people more than once. If their dignity is left in tact, they'll talk and in most cases provide good information.

I used a scenario to teach new officers before they met the public. It is as real as life can be.

While on patrol an officer observes a station wagon going down the road with a loud exhaust. The officer stops the vehicle. The first observation is a male driver, female passenger and three children in the back seat. The exhaust is loud and obviously faulty.

The officer approaches the vehicle and askes the driver for a license, registration, and insurance card. The driver hands the officer a license, registration and says he doesn't have the insurance card.

A quick look at the vehicle reveals that the muffler is gone. The man is operating a vehicle with a faulty exhaust system. What do you do? Nearly every officer answers: Write him a ticket.

A check of the license and registration reveals that the registration expired a month ago. The man is operating an unregistered motor vehicle.

What do you do? Nearly all the new officers answer the same; arrest the operator.

Further examination of the vehicle reveals that the inspection sticker expired a month ago. What do you do? Nearly ever officer answers; write him a ticket.

At this point these officers have arrested the man and ticketed two other violations, all without ever talking to the driver.

The unknown facts are that the man has his wife and family with him in the vehicle. He lost his job a month ago and is on his was home from the unemployment office, where he was seeking new employment.

However, these new officers didn't take the time to learn any of this information, they just arrested the man in front of his wife and family.

Two days later, the arresting officer is called to a burglary scene.

As he is doing the neighborhood canvas, he walks up to a house right in sight of the burglarized home and knocks on the door. Who comes to the door, the man he arrested two days before, in front of the man's family, for operating an unregistered vehicle. This man's dignity was just swept from him by this officer just two days ago. What do you think he's going to tell the officer about what he observed from his window?

The point here is not to let motor vehicle violations pass but to be tactful. The situation could have been handled in several different ways. The obvious follow up is; What did the officer leave for an impression with the man's wife and children?

My last tool is not to let anyone use my uniform or me for their gain. When I start a new class of officers, I always ask them to describe what the badge means to them in five words or less. I have a formula for the answer; 95% and 5%. 95% of the officers answer with the words "POWER and/or ARREST. The remaining generally offer "SERVE & PROTECT."

The answer I'm looking for is: <u>A SYMBOL OF PUBLIC TRUST</u>. That answer implies that an officer should never allow anyone to tarnish that badge.

It was the first evening of the Cornish Fair. I had three brand new officers that had completed their training and were ready to meet the public. I had given them instructions to be at the Fair Ground at six that afternoon to stand inspection with the Chief and the Sheriff.

They were spotless and the cruisers were polished to perfection. As the new men were standing inspection I spotted a man followed by a substantial entourage of photographers. He was headed right for us. Not wanting the man to interrupt the inspection I headed him off.

I recognized the man as a Congressman from Maine. The man quickly threw an arm over my shoulder and the cameras were clicking fast and furiously. It was obvious to me that the man saw a photo op and jumped on it. By doing so he had put me on the spot. I had given the new officers my lecture about not allowing the uniform to be used by anyone.

As the camera were clicking, the Congressman standing with an arm on my shoulder, I asked him what his opinion of the Clinton scandal was, He replied, "It's gone on much too long, hasn't it?" Well that sharpened the arrow real quickly. He offered a question in answer to my question. So I asked him, "Do you know the tragedy of that situation?" He answered "No, tell me." So with cameras clicking and note pads at every quarter I replied, " Clinton didn't do anything to that gal that you haven't be doing to the taxpayers in Maine since you've been elected." End of photo op, good bye Mr. Congressman, thanks for stopping.

None of the photos that were taken were ever published in the area papers. So, the man didn't use my uniform. I set the example for the new officers. That's not to say that the Chief, Sheriff and for that matter, the new officers weren't laughing. Mr. Congressman was pissed.

It was a typical winter day in Maine. I was second in a line of vehicles behind a school bus. In front of me was a Trooper that was working commercial vehicle enforcement. The bus stopped on Rt 202, at the Bennett Road intersection to let students off the bus.

A motorcycle came out of the Bennett Road, without stopping, popped a wheelie, cut a circle, sending sand and rocks at the bus. The male operating the motorcycle then saw two police vehicles behind the bus.

He spun the motor cycle around and fled down a snowmobile trail that was near the intersection. The students got off the bus and the bus left. The Trooper left as well. I pulled in to Bennett Road and parked my cruiser.

I got out and listened. I couldn't hear the motorcycle. Realizing that there was two feet of snow on the ground, and the snowmobile trail was only about two feet wide, my guess was Mr. Sleezy rider was off the trail snowbound.

Aware that this young man pulled his stunt, in front of a busload of high school students, I could not allow the uniform to be soiled.

My patrol zone was very rural. During the winter I always had a set of snowshoes in the trunk. I knew the motorcycle was not far away or I would have heard it. I put the snowshoes on and advised dispatch of my location and that I was in pursuit of a motorcycle on snowshoes.

I didn't realize how that sounded over the police radio at the time. I just started following the motorcycle tracks. I went about three hundred yards into the woods and there he was. Sleezy Rider was off the trail, trying to push that motorcycle through the snow.

It only took a matter of a minute or two to overtake him. I took the snowshoes off and after a moment of denial, Sleezy Rider came in second in our altercation, and was arrested.

I was only to learn later that Sleezy's license was under suspension, and he was a habitual offender, making the crime a felony. I simply did what I had to do in that situation.

And now, the rest of the story!

It seems that a news reporter was in his vehicle and heard me say that I was in foot pursuit of a motorcycle on snowshoes. He followed the radio conversation and knew I had arrested the man within five minutes of the chase.

He wrote the story for his paper; Deputy Gets His Man. AP picked up the story and the next morning, the story was on Paul Harvey News. A foolish thing like that makes national news. Burglary cases that took hard police work and months to solve, never got more than local attention. You just can't figure it out.

I took more doo-doo for that arrest from the local law enforcement community than I care to mention. The simple fact is, police officers don't get paid to finish second.

The tool here was tenacity.

The Truth,
And
Nothing But
The Truth

As a police officer, your integrity, and that of your Department, must be maintained at the highest level. Every officer is responsible for himself/herself and the Department. Bad cops make it hard for the good ones.

Early on in my career, I watched courtroom trials with an objective eye. Over the course of a few months, I began to notice a few patterns. The trials always seemed to involve the same officers. I listened to officers give testimony that sounded like a record playing. I watched Defendants reactions to the officer's testimony.

I would stand around in the halls after a trial and hear the Defendants talk about how the officer lied in the courtroom. To be honest, you expect some of that. However, when I kept hearing it, I began to wonder. I want to point out that these officers were not from my Department. District Court's in Maine, handle several Departments.

I began to think about how much I really knew about my fellow officers within my own Department. The more I thought, the more I realized that my integrity was on the line with everyone that wore the same uniform I did. After some thought, I came up with an idea.

Integrity is as basic as black and white, there is no compromise. Either a man is honest or he isn't. I reason that both taking something that does not belong to you and the act of lying are acts that a person knows as being wrong at the outset. The person committing the act knows it to be wrong in his/her heart. To me this is a basic tenant.

I came up with a plan to leave a quarter on a table top and observe who in my Department would take it from the table and pocket it. I did the same thing in the locker room of the correction people. I lost a few of quarters but gained a wealth of information about the integrity of my fellow Deputies. I must say the majority didn't take the quarter, but I was stunned by how many that did.

That information came in very handy later on when I was doing internal affairs investigations. I could ask the question; "Did you ever take money that didn't belong to you?" I knew the truth and the person I was asking didn't know I knew. I had a very good reputation for finding the truth. I never showed my list to anybody, but when push came to shove, the polygraph always substantiated my findings. All for the price of a quarter. Think about it.

Lawyers are like police officers, some have integrity and some never heard the word. I never needed a thermometer to tell me how cold it was in Maine. You can tell when it's cold in Maine; all the lawyers have their hands in their own pockets. I've met some great lawyers and some really bad ones.

A police officer should understand that a conviction from a court of law is where the officer's role ends. An officer should never get hung up on fine amounts or sentences. Believe it or not, politics has a lot to do with the plea bargain process, which is out of the officer's control.

When the DA's office starts trading it's like the stock exchange. The truth is, a defense attorney will fight for a deal with a client that has paid cash, but be more inclined to trade off cases that are frequent flyers and never pay the lawyer. Lawyer's have to make a living too.

I used to watch the process and I was just amazed at the

process of observing the wheels of justice in motion. What a show! Sometimes I actually felt sorry for the Defendants.

I had my own classification system for lawyers. I'm proud to say there were more good than bad. Some became good friends and some I wouldn't trust to carry guts to a bear.

The first class was just that, pure class, very professional at every turn. They had a good grasp on reality and were always satisfied with a fair deal. They represented their clients well and they were a pleasure to work with.

The second class was the piss and moan class. Never satisfied, always wanting more. These folks usually wound up in trials and not winning very many cases. They usually lied more than their clients.

The third class was the Wild Bill class. Most of these hadn't read a law book since Wild Bill was a Sheriff. Hey, some of these guys probably played cards with Wild Bill.

Let me make it clear that I was never hung up on what came out of the courtroom. I did my part and the rest was out of my control. My record of convictions was very high. I didn't care what the fine or sentence was, that was a matter for the courts to decide.

Several years ago, Maine went to a bucks only hunting season. New Hampshire was still a state where either sex deer were legal. Rod Small, a Game Warden, asked me to spend a little time with him on a back woods road that lead into New Hampshire on the first day of a deer hunting season. He felt that with the new Bucks only law, folks might kill a doe and transport it over the state line into New Hampshire, and register it as a legal kill in that state.

We met and parked out in the woods. We never got a game violation. We did however, make two vehicle stops. Both were pickup trucks coming into Maine from New Hampshire. One truck had thirty cases of beer and the other had twenty cases of beer. The beer was seized and I wrote summonses to the operators for the violations.

The Defendants appeared in court for trial represented by an attorney. Their lawyer got the DA so pissed off that the DA wanted to take the case to trial. I recall that the potential fine was very high. I think it was $500 per case over the limit of one case per person.

O.K. These guys were not what I would want for hunting buds, but they weren't hard core criminals either. The attorney told them what the fine was going to be and that the case was headed to trial. One of the Defendants came to me and told me he didn't have that kind of money and he was really scared. I told him I'd talk to the DA. I got the attorney and we went into the DA's office for a second go-around. The attorney started pissing and moaning and I finally asked him to leave the office, much to the amazement of the DA.

I told the man that he hadn't read a law book since he helped write letters for Sam Houston. I talked with the DA and the Defendants pled, each paid two hundred dollars, and the rest of the fine was suspended. They were nice guys, but I wouldn't hunt with them.

I was at District Court one morning for an operating under the influence trial. This man introduced himself to me as lawyer representing the man I had arrested. He told me that he wasn't going to trial with the case, he would plead the man, as the evidence was really quite strong.

The trial was scheduled for the afternoon so I left the courthouse and returned home. Something told me to return to the courthouse so I went back and took a seat in the rear of the courtroom. The afternoon list was called with a DA, Defendants and attorneys and each side either agreed to a plea or the case went to trial that day.

When my O.U.I. case was called, the attorney immediately moved for dismissal as the arresting office was not present for trial. I stood up in the rear of the courtroom. The Judge, seeing me standing, pointed to me to speak. I replied " Your Honor, the arresting office is present." That pathetic attorney did a 180 and there I was.

The attorney immediately retracted his statement and informed the Judge that that case was to be plead. The Judge wasn't stupid, he knew what was going on. The Judge took the plea right then, pasted sentence and the case was over. The Judge called for a recess. I got called into chambers before the Judge. He asked me what happened and I told him.

The attorney was called into chambers after me. I don't know what was said but I do know that attorney never defended another of my arrestees. My guess is he didn't have to strain for a bowel movement for a while. Forever after, when I saw the man in the courthouse I made a point of saying, "You can always tell when a lawyer is lying, his lips are moving." I can't understand, he never came into the back room with the other attorneys and police officers to chat.

Early on in my career, Pam Lawrason, taught me the ropes of case preparation. One point she made clear was that the time lapse from arrest to trial could be from three months to a year. She made the point that I should always request an extra booking photo and include the photo in my original report. The reason is that the report must be made available to the Defense and is known as discovery.

The more important fact is that on trial day, the officer has a reference photo to help identify the Defendant. I used the photo and even went one step further. I would talk to the Defendant before the trial always saying that I wish things had turned out better. I couldn't give a hoot in hell what the Defendant's reply was but I listened to his speech pattern. I got what I wanted.

I had a trial in Superior Court for a guy who had two previous convictions for O.U.I. I spoke with the Defendant before the trial and he was well educated and rather articulate.

I was called into the courtroom and after being sworn in I took the stand.

The DA did the usual job on direct questioning and made all the points of the case. Then the Defense Attorney started to put on his show. When he got to the slurred speech part of the report, he established that I didn't know the Defendant. Then asked how I knew that he didn't speak with a slur?

My answer was, " You know Sir, I was wondering the same thing. So I spoke to your client this morning in the hall and he was really quite articulate, unlike the night of the arrest."

That ended that line of questioning really quickly. Then he asked if I could identify the Defendant. I replied, "Yes." He asked, "Isn't that him seated at the defense table?" I answered, "NO!" The attorney went into a spiel claiming that I couldn't identify the Defendant. He then instructed me to identify the man seated at the defense table. I might point out that the DA didn't have a clue what was going on. I answered, "I have no idea who the man seated at the table is but the Defendant is seated in the next to the last row on the right side, wearing a black suit and a blue tie."

The man was convicted, and the attorney eventually was disbarred. Not for that case but for other stuff he pulled.

I recall a young attorney receiving a court appointment one morning at District Court. As I was leaving the courtroom, the attorney called his new client outside. Standing in the hallway, the attorney asked the man, " Is this your first time being a shithead or have you always be a shithead?" Hey, some attorneys catch on real quick.

Most DA's are average attorney but there are few like Pam Lawarson. She was one hell of an attorney. Most are right out of law school. I made a habit of researching case law and knowing what I was doing, thanks to Pam.

In later years, the DA's office was packed with young kids that couldn't get a disorderly conduct conviction on Jack the Ripper if they had a signed confession. I've been known to call a spade a spade. When one of them started to hem and haw I'd end it real quick. I'd tell them that if the hadn't finished lower than whale shit in their law class, they'd be in a good firm making money.

I got a call one day to meet with the actual District Attorney to discuss a plea agreement. When I walked in she and the Defense Attorney were seated.

The case involved the arrest of a Trooper's son for drug trafficking. I had two controlled buys and netted a marijuana growing operation, cocaine, and a large sum of money.

The DA told me that she was going to asked for 90 days jail time, stay the sentence until late September and return property and money. She had the gall to ask me what I thought. I told her that I though it was a very generous solution and suggested that she formalize the papers for a three way partnership between her, the defendant and the defense attorney. I noted that since she was putting him back in business she must be interested in the profits.

She blew a gasket and I walked out. The defendant didn't get his money, or equipment back and he did six months in jail. The bottom line here was politics pure and simple. The Defense Attorney was a big party guy and the DA was looking for support. Don't think it don't happen baby, cause it does.

I was working a road check with a Trooper on Rt 25 in Limington one morning. The Trooper had one lane and I took the other. I motioned this big Buick to the side as the inspection sticker was expired by six months. I approached the vehicle and asked for a license and registration. The registration had expired almost a year before.

I explained to the operator that the vehicle was unregistered. I issued a ticket for the registration violation and looked up to see the Trooper leaving. He called me by radio and asked me if I knew who I had stopped? I replied, "So and so, date of birth xx/xx/xx`." The Trooper said no more.

I returned to the vehicle and gave the operator a ticket and a permit to operate the vehicle to the registry. The man signed the ticket and said, "I'll see you in court." I thought nothing of the statement, as you hear that all the time.

Two days later, I was on that same road in Limington about eleven in the evening. I received notification from dispatch that an armed robbery had just happened in the town of Ossippee, New Hanpshire. The vehicle description was given as well as the fact that the vehicle had Maine plates and was last seen headed toward Maine. Translated, the vehicle was coming my way.

I knew it would take that vehicle about thirty minutes to reach me so I used the time to get more information. There were three male subjects in the vehicle. They had used ski masks and were armed with handguns. I called for backup and two Troopers started toward my location but were twenty or more minutes away.

I stopped the vehicle and the Troopers arrived within seconds.

The three were arrested. Guns, masks and the money bag were on the front floor of the vehicle in plain sight. About as straight forward as you can get.

All three were transported to the county jail and charged with a fugitive from justice charge.

In Maine, people can not sit in a jail more than 48 hours without arraignment. Since the arrest was made on a Thursday night, they were going to be arraigned in Biddeford District Court the next morning.

I arrived at the Biddeford District Court and walked into the courtroom. I recognized the Judge immediately as the man I had ticketed just that week for an unregistered motor vehicle. I stopped dead in my tracks. The Judge looked at me and declared "RECESS."

Not more than a minute later, The Bailiff came up to me and said that the Judge wanted to see me. OH SHIT! I walked into chambers and the Judge invited me/ told me to sit. He looked at me and said, "I don't ever want to see you walk into my courtroom with that look on your face again. You did your job, very professionally I might add, and I'm proud to have officers like you out there. However, I can assure you that Trooper X, the gutless bastard, won't get the same greeting." The Judge then pulled a receipt out of his desk and showed me that he had already paid the fine and the vehicle was registered and inspected.

I was at home one day and my wife called me from the Superior Court where she worked. She told me that a lawyer had traveled from Houlton, Maine to defend a man I had arrested a few days before. She told me that he wanted to dispose of the case while he was here so I agreed to meet him at the courthouse.

We sat down on a bench at the end of the hall and he started asking questions. I could see where it was going so I stopped the conversation real quick. I explained that I didn't know the guy from Adam. I explained that when I investigated a case I started them all the same way. I listed all the hits, runs and errors for both sides. At the end of the game, if probable cause exists, I make the arrest, if it doesn't, case closed.

He went on to say that the defendant was related to him. He said that he had just spoken with him and he was insistent that he didn't do the crime. I replied, that he might re-interview his client, and I'd be available should he want a trial.

He went back to the jail and his client admitted the crime to him. He pled the man in Superior Court and went to the Clerk's office to complete the necessary paperwork. He noticed my wife's name and asked her if she was related to me. She told him that she was my wife. The man told her that he was impressed that he had met an honest cop.

That attorney became our next Attorney General for the State of Maine.

There are good one's out there.

I received a call from a Game Warden friend to meet with him. He had something on his mind and finally he came out with it. It seems that he had just left District Court. Court wasn't in session and he had stopped to find out the status of a case he had.

The Warden had summoned a man for fishing without a license. The case was five months old. The man hadn't paid his fine. The usual process for this is that the Clerk of the District Court would issue an arrest warrant for failure to pay a fine. That is generally done after a couple of months.

When the Warden asked the status of the case, the Clerk answered that the man had called that morning and said he would be in and pay his fine that week. The Clerk, was to put it mildly, a bitch. She ran that Clerk's office with an iron hand and gave any officer she didn't like a very rough time. That included most all the officers in the area, especially me.

The Game Warden wasn't in her good graces either. I thought about it for a minute or two and asked the Warden to ride with me. I asked him to look at the address on his summons. I decided we'd pay the man a visit. We arrived at the residence and rang the doorbell and a man answered the door. The Warden asked the man if he was going to settle the fine and the man said he would take care of it on Friday when he got paid.

The Warden was satisfied, thanked the man and started to walk away. I asked the man, "When did the Clerk call you?" He replied, "She just called, I was talking to her when you arrived." I responded, "Oh I though you called her." He answered, "No, the matter just slipped my mind."

Not only did the Clerk lie, she hindered the process as well. The Warden was really pissed. He filed a formal complaint. That Clerk had been at that court since dirt, and thought she was God. Well, she found out that God rested after making the heavens and earth because she got time off without pay.

HAVE
AT IT

It seems that in every Sheriff's Department there are Corrections Officers that just know their destiny is to be a cruiser jockey. My Department was no exception.

I had the mindset that we all wore the same uniform. I tried to help out at the jail when they needed it and had built a good relationship with the jail boys. It didn't help that the majority of our Patrol Deputies looked down on the Corrections guys. I had a standing offer that the Corrections guys were welcome to join me on patrol anytime.

The prevailing attitude among the Corrections guys was that anyone could do patrol, it was easy. I gave them a chance to find out just how easy it was. They all shared one common thought. Write tickets and show em' who's in charge.

A Corrections Deputy asked if he could ride with me at the end of his jail shift and I told him I'd love to have him. I arrived at the jail right at four in the afternoon. The man had to get his gun-belt from his locker and he was ready to go. I need to explain the Corrections Officers do not carry weapons in the jail. Jail regulation required that weapons be secured in the several gun lockers in the car port of the jail. Everyone is required to deposit their weapon in a locker before entering the jail.

The man came out of the locker room buckling his belt and he was ready to go. I asked him if he wanted to drive. Yee Ha, we were off to the rodeo.

We traveled into the Shapleigh area on Rt 11. There were a lot of seasonal people in that area and speed limit signs didn't mean much so I thought it would be a good place to start. He parked at the Shapleigh Dump entrance. There was a good view of the road, both ways, and the cruiser was visible. After all, the objective is to enhance voluntary compliance.

I explained the operation of the radar gun. Pulling the trigger once, locks the target's speed. The second pull releases the lock and the gun will read zero. I then explained that by sound alone, within a matter of a few vehicles you could tell when a speeder was coming. He applied that rocket science and within a few vehicles he was right on the money and proud of his accomplishment.

Then a "cooker" came along. He was cookin' at 75mph in a 50 zone. My pard, pointed the radar gun and started pulling the trigger. That trigger was going like a trip-hammer. As the cooker passed by my pard threw the radar gun at me. It hit me in the knee and hurt like hell.

He started the cruiser, slammed it into gear and the chase was on. The first thing he said to me was, "He's getting away, he's not going to stop. I'll call in a pursuit." I casually put my hand over the mic so that he wouldn't reach for it. I then asked if he realized that we were going 65mph in low gear. I instructed him to take his foot off the accelerator and shift the vehicle into drive.

He started to gain on the cooker and then told me again that he wasn't going to stop. I looked at him and said, "He probably won't stop until you put the front blue lights on, you've got the rear blues on, not the front. I reached over and put the right switch on. The cooker pulled over right away.

My pard got out of the cruiser and approached the vehicle. As he approached the vehicle he realized his holster was empty. I watched as he got the required license and registration. As he was walking back to the cruiser, I looked down at the radar gun. It read zero.

My pard got into the cruiser and ran the usual license check and reached for the summons book. I suggested that before he wrote the ticket, he invite the driver back to see the radar. He thought that was a god idea and started to get out. I called him back and told him he might want to look at the gun before he invited the driver back. He looked at the gun and said, I haven't done anything right on this whole thing. The driver got a warning for speed.

After we cleared the stop, my pard decided he'd had enough as he was tired from the day's work at the jail. It took about a half-hour to get back to the jail. He got out of the cruiser and thanked me. As he was walking away, I said, "Don't forget your weapon in the weapon locker." He replied, "Damn, you don't miss nothing do ya?" He never asked to patrol again. He was a good Corrections man and I never discussed his patrol career with anyone in the Department. Dignity is important to every man.

A Corrections Officer from the second shift asked to patrol with me after he got off at midnight. I picked him up and we were off like a prom dress.

My bud didn't want to drive, just observe.

The Town of Alfred had just had the first stop-light in the town installed. It had been operating for about a month at a dangerous intersection. There had been several fatal crashes at that intersection.

We parked at a gas station, adjacent to the intersection. The cruiser stood out like a naked lady in a Baptist Choir on Sunday morning. We watched the intersection and I explained to my bud, how I applied the law. If the light was red, and I observed a vehicle go through the light, the operator of the vehicle established his own destiny. If I saw brake lights come on, the operator got a warning. No brake lights, the operator got a summons.

We issued a couple of warnings and we continued to observe the intersection. A vehicle approached the intersection and never attempted to stop. There was no appearance of brake lights at all. I stopped the vehicle.

My bud had lived in the Alfred/Lyman area for years and knew everybody, including the operator of the vehicle. The lady was the Chairwoman of the Selectmen's Board in the Town of Alfred.

I wrote the lady a ticket and explained that she made no attempt to stop or slow down while at the intersection. My bud was so nervous that I had summonsed a Selectperson that he had to go home. Hey, some people don't make good umpires. His patrol career was over.

I was patrolling one summer evening with a Reserve Deputy. We were in Sanford getting fuel when we heard a Trooper call in a pursuit chase. The Trooper described the vehicle as a roadrunner with a Dixie flag painted on the trunk. I knew the vehicle and I knew that the operator lived on the Stagecoach Road in Parsonsfield.

We arrived in Parsonsfield while the Trooper was still involved with the pursuit. I head the Trooper say that the vehicle had taken a woods road. That road led through a small corner of Wakefield, New Hampshire. The Wakefield police had set up a roadblock. They were located about two miles from where we were parked.

It had taken nearly a half hour for us to get to the area. The man's residence was in sight. I realized that we had to stop the vehicle before reaching the residence as I wanted to avoid a barricade situation.

The Trooper then radioed that he was stuck in the mud on the woods road and that the road-runner was negotiating the road well as it had wide tires.

The Reserve Deputy that was my pard for the night, was a Captain in the Air Force and was stationed at a nearby airbase. He was a pilot and very cool under pressure. In fact, I have to say, that this man was the best Reserve Deputy the Department ever had.

I explained that we were in a good position to back up Wakefield and if the man ran the Wakefield boys we'd have our chance. He was quick to observe that the roads were rather narrow. I got the shotgun from the trunk and as I got back into the vehicle the Wakefield boys advised that he had just ran their block. It was up to us.

I parked the cruiser, with light on, in the narrow road and instructed the Deputy to go down the road fifty feet or so and take a position on the right side of the road, in the woods, as no one would suspect him there.

We heard the vehicle coming at us. I left enough room for the vehicle to get by the cruiser, just as I was taught. I stood slightly behind my cruiser. As the vehicle came toward me, I jacked a round into the chamber of the shotgun. I was standing facing the left-hand ditch, so that my action with the shotgun was in the operator's view. Then I swung the shotgun right at the vehicle.

The vehicle came to a stop real quick. I instructed the operator to get out of the vehicle, and lay face down in the road. The Reserve Deputy came out of the woods and cuffed the man. Chase over!

The operator was wearing an Air Force uniform. He was less than pleased that he was so close to home and got caught. He was less than polite, in short, he was a butt-hole. He gave the Reserve Deputy a full ration of shit, playing the real tough guy role to the hilt.

The Trooper that was pursuing this man, got picked up by another Trooper.

They arrived at the scene about ten minutes after the arrest. They transported the man to jail and we left the area.

As we were driving down the road the Reserve Deputy said to me, "If that Airman gets out of jail, he'll shit tomorrow." I asked why. The Reserve told me that he was the Base Duty Officer the next day and that that Airman would have to report to him. He said, "He'll get a lot more than he gave me tonight."

The point here is that by knowing my patrol zone, I knew where that vehicle was going. In Maine you just don't see very many vehicles with a Confederate flag painted on them. Having knowledge of the roads, where the vehicle belonged, and the Trooper giving location and direction of travel, I realized it was only a matter of time.

I had a pard for a couple of years. He was an older man who just loved to ride along. He was the Constable for the town of Shapleigh. In Maine, many towns have a "Dog Officer". Now the new buzz word is "Animal Control Officer". Charlie Timmons was a great man. Dedicated to his wife Gladys, who was confined to bed for several years. He would answer "dog complaints" in town but spent the majority of each day as a homebody caring for his wife. During the evenings he got away and chose to ride with me.

Charlie was a retired bus driver from the Boston area. He was also a WWII vet. He served in the Army Air Corp. He was as proud a MIC as one ever saw. He eventually became a Reserve Deputy. Charlie past away a few years ago. I miss him as a friend, and though his police career was short, he was a good officer and I was proud to call him a friend and fellow officer.

Although Charlie wasn't versed in all areas of the profession, when the chips were down, he did the right things. One of his few short suits was demeanor on the radio. By his own admission, he didn't give a damn who was listening, he gave it straight and clear.

Province Lake Beach is located in Parsonsfield. It's a really nice, sandy beach that runs for nearly half a mile along RT 153. During the summer evenings, every year, I got open fire complaints from that beach. I need to explain that the area though rural, is heavily wooded and a fire would spread real fast. Province Lake Beach is on the New Hampshire line and about forty minutes travel time from the Sheriff's Office, on a good day.

I had been to Province Lake Beach five Fridays in a row to respond to open fire complaints. Each Friday I issued warnings to the folks responsible for the open fires. I explained that if the fires continued, I would issue summonses. I realized that these folks were on vacation and I didn't want to spoil their vacations with a court summons.

Week six came and I received a complaint of open fires on Province Lake Beach. Charlie was riding with me. I had alerted the Forest Wardens of the situation on the Beach during the weeks leading up to this night. They were awaiting my call. I had Charlie notify them through our dispatch as I was headed for the Beach.

When we arrived there were several fires on the beach, I can't recall just how many, eight or ten I guess. I told Charlie that my plan was that I would start at the New Hampshire line, walk up the entire beach and arrest the responsible person for each fire. Charlie would drive the cruiser along with me and seat the arrestees for the ride back to the county jail.

I started up the beach and began arresting folks. The Forest Warden hadn't arrived yet. I had arrested several, after each arrest Charlie would notify dispatch of another prisoner. The radio procedure is quite simple just a call number, in this case, County 11, 10-46. As I walked along the beach the number of "10-46's rose to eight or ten. Dispatch realized that the number of prisoners was becoming very large.

After Charlie had reached eight or nine, dispatch asked, "How is County 11 going to transport that many prisoners?" Charlie was very intent on watching the arrested people that I had walked to the cruiser. He was all business, which is as it should be. He answered, "I don't know County, maybe he'll put em' in the god damn trunk for all I know, we're up to our ass in prisoners here, I'll get back to you." I think everybody in the world was listening to their scanners that night because the whole world knew that County 11 had a round up on the beach in Parsonsfield.

The Forest Warden arrived and we loaded three into my cruiser, and the rest into the back of the Forest Warden's pickup and transported them to the jail.

In Shapleigh there is a Game Preserve named after a career Game Warden who lived in and patrolled Shapleigh for years. The man's name was Vernon Walker. Within that area there is a pond called Spicer Pond. The pond is loaded with small brook trout. Fishing in that pond is limited to artificial lures only.

I noticed several motor vehicles parked outside the gate one morning so Charlie and I decided to walk down to the pond and see what was going on. As we approached the pond we could see people fishing.

One man had three young boys with him and they were fishing in the brook, the outlet of the pond. The man was busy putting worms on the kids hooks and generally helping the kids. The kids weren't catching anything and were insistent that they wanted to fish in the pond on the other side of the road.

There was a single man fishing in the pond. He was catching trout. We watched without being detected for about a half-hour. The Fish and Game people had clearly posted several signs around the pond with the regulation for fishing the pond. (artificial lures only) We observed the single man catching trout, all very small, and putting them on a stick, hiding them under a rock. All being illegal as hell. All the while, the kids were watching, catching nothing in the brook, and wanting to fish in the pond. Of course, Dad, knowing that fishing with worms in the pond wasn't legal, encouraged the kids to fish in the brook.

After we had watched long enough, we walked out in plain sight and approached all the fishermen. While talking to the boys, the single man started to walk off. Realizing that the boys had been tempted, and Dad had not allowed them to fish in the pond, I asked the single man to see his fishing license.

He denied fishing in the pond, saying he had just gotten there. I turned over the rock, and collected a stick with a dozen small trout, all less than the minimum size limit. Then walked to where he was fishing and picked up his container of worms.

The man squealed like a stuck pig while I wrote the summons. I took my time. I wanted the kids to see a violator getting what he so justly deserved.

After the violator left, very unhappy, we complimented the boys on their sportsmanship.

Later during deer hunting season, Charlie and I were on patrol. We had turned onto a back road and saw a bunch of vehicles parked. The hunters were out in force. Charlie saw a hunter moving through the woods so we stopped. It was our old friend the fisherman who liked catching short trout with worms.

It seemed that he liked venison because he was dragging two small deer.

In Maine, one deer is the limit. He lost his deer, got another summons, this time from Charlie.

Charlie had been around me too much. He said to the man, "I'll bet you're just dragging the second one out for a friend." The man eagerly responded that he was doing just that. Charlie, walked up an inspected both deer. A hunter is required to place a tag on a deer before moving it from the point where it was killed. Neither deer had a tag. Charlie now realizes that he has two violations.

Charlie then asked the man, "Do you have the rest of the week off to hunt?" The man responded, "Yes, I do." Charlie said, "Good, you won't miss work while you're in jail, you are under arrest." The man started to complain about how life wasn't fair as Charlie was applying the handcuffs.

Then Charlie responded with one of my lines, "Ya, times are tough, even the subways are in the hole." I was laughing my ass off. "Oh God what have I done," Charlie is coming into his own. (I miss you, pard) I was on patrol one Friday evening and the Sheriff was riding with me. From time to time, he would ride with me or the Chief. During the week he was generally busy with meetings, budgets or politics, but the man always cared about his people. When he'd had enough bull shit he'd get down in the trenches with us. Hell, if we had a marijuana field he'd be out there pulling and lugging plants just like the rest of us.

I received a call to assist a motorist on the Shady Nook Road in Newfield, Maine. When I received the call I was in Limington. I was a half-hour away if I leaned on it. It took us about that much time to get there.

I turned onto the Shady Nook Road and traveled about a half mile and we came upon a relatively new Caddie with a Mass. registration. I parked the cruiser behind the Caddie and got out. The Sheriff remained in the cruiser to sign us off at the complaint.

A tall man in his sixties got out and walked toward me shouting, "Where the hell have you's guys been? When I calls the cops in Boston, they're there in five minutes." All the while he is poking his finger in my chest. He went on to say "I gives five-hundred bucks a year to the cops Benevolent Association and they are always there in five minutes to change a tire for me."

Let me tell you, the first time he put his finger in my chest, I decided to use the dull arrow because they hurt more. After he finished talking, I asked if he was through. He answered, "Ya, Ya, Ya." I reached into my pocket and pulled out a quarter. I said, "Here you are sir," handing him the quarter. The man looked at me and said," What ta hell is this for?" Being the kind and gentle officer that I was, I put my finger on his chest and replied, "Call the Boston Cops," returned to the cruiser and left waving good-bye as we left. I thought the Sheriff was going to piss himself laughing.

The Sheriff was C. Wesley Phinney. I can best describe him in the words of Othelo; "A Good and Honest Man." He knew his people and he was loyal to them.

I had been working on a burglary investigation for twenty-four straight hours and had developed information that the burglar had gone to a small town in Connecticut.

The correct procedure was to obtain authorization from the DA's office before issuing a teletype in interstate cases. I got the authorization and contacted the local police department in Connecticut. Within ten minutes they had the burglar and the entire $28,000 worth of stolen property. Case closed! WRONG!

While I went home for a few hours sleep, the District Attorney and the Sheriff had a pissing contest over the cost of rendition and the DA refused to authorize bringing the man back to Maine.

I returned to the office a few hours later to find out the news. I could see that it was a basic R's vs D's political deal. I was adamant that professional law enforcement was not going to play second fiddle to politics.

I called the DA at home and asked his advice. I explained that I had a problem and I didn't know what to do about it. The DA asked me what the problem was. I told him that I didn't know what to do first. He said, "Why don't you start by telling me what the problem is?" I replied, "Here's my problem, I've worked for twenty-four straight hours to solve a $28,000 burglary, only to find out that you won't go get the guy. So my problem is, do I get an arrest warrant for you for malfeasance of office, or do I give the victim your home telephone number and let you explain your position to him."

The DA responded, "I have to make these decisions all the time, it's nothing personal." I replied, "Well it's nothing personal with me, why don't I let the Portland Press Herald in on your decision, I'm sure they'll be interested."

The DA called the Sheriff and the burglar was brought back

to Maine. Several weeks later, The DA after my neck, requested a meeting, with the Sheriff, him and I. The Sheriff spent a good hour before the meeting explaining to me that my best approach was to be quiet and condescending. We arrived at the DA's office and he invited us to have a seat. I looked him right square in the eye and said, " Ever since you've been the DA, I've thought you to be an asshole, now is your time to say something that will change my mind."

After a few brief minutes the meeting ended. While walking out the door a thought struck me. I turned, looked at the man and said, "You know something just came to me. I was a Deputy Sheriff before you were elected DA, and I'll be a Deputy Sheriff the day you leave."

The day that DA left the Courthouse for the last time as DA, I opened the door for him and as he walked out I said, "I'm still a Deputy Sheriff, have a good day."

We were at the range one day and I was looking to qualify and get out of there as soon as I could. The Sheriff's Department had become a kind of regional firearms qualification center. That complicated qualification as it took much longer.

The Range Master was explaining to some shooters that a perfect target would have all fifty bullets in the ten-ring. He was very insistent on that point and took great pain to make his point. He was in charge and he wanted them to know it. Well, as he was pounding his point home I was sharpening my arrow.

I went to the line and got ready to shoot. I was shooting a .45 caliber semi-auto.

I was on the number five target. The man beside me, on the number four target was shooting a .357 caliber weapon.

After I finished my first station, I had a large hole shot out of the ten-ring of my target. When I finished my second station the hole in my target was about three inches in diameter. I had worked to enlarge the hole and I was successful. At my third station, I began to shoot a nose, eyes and lips on the head of the number four target.

When the shooting ended, the Range Master started at target

one, counted the bullet holes and scored the target, then moving on down the line. When he got to the number four target he counted sixty-five bullet holes. He knew that there is only a total of fifty shoots. He re-counted the target and again reached a total of sixty-five. Then he realized the size of the holes in the head.

He walked over to my target and saw a large hole in the ten-ring, looked at me and said, "Gentlemen, I've just been had." I replied, "All you have to do is prove that all fifty shots didn't go right through that hole, otherwise, it's a perfect target."

IF YA WANT
TO RUN WITH
THE BIG DOGS
YOU GOT
TO GET OFF
THE PORCH

There are many dedicated professionals in the law enforcement community. The desire to become part of that great and noble corps is commendable in and of itself. I have said it before and I'll say it again, "LAW ENFORCEMENT IS NOT A JOB, IT'S A WAY OF LIFE."

I'd like to impart what I believe are the necessary attributes of a good police officer. There is a time to laugh and a time to be serious. Here is my serious side.

BE A PART OF YOUR COMMUNITY. Never set yourself apart from the community you serve. Once an officer looses empathy for the public, the officer looses the capacity to be effective in the community.

Half of communication is being a good listener. Listen to the issues that the community is concerned about. Apply yourself to be a part of the answer and not a part of the problem.

Become involved with community functions, and be accessible. When an officer talks with the public, they will talk to the officer. Youth activities, civic events, or church activities are always a good starting point. Setting a positive example for the next generation lays the groundwork for a successful career and a better community. A child should have no better role model than a police officer.

PROTECT YOURSELF AND YOUR DEPARTMENT FROM INCOMPETANCE AND MEDIOCRACY. Standing up for right is very difficult, and often lonesome at best. Each officer must go out into the community every day and prove him/herself within the community as being worthy of that community's trust.

There is nothing better than setting high standards for an officer's department. A good officer only wants to be surrounded by other good officers. One bad apple spoils the whole barrel.

An officer should never allow his badge to be tarnished by the words or deeds of another officer. The officer has a responsibility to him/herself and the department to take corrective action. The public often judges the department by the words or deeds of one officer. It then becomes paramount for all officers within that department to be held to the same high standards.

One bad attitude, one stupid comment at a wrong time, reflects on the entire department and the profession. Expect and accept nothing less than total professionalism, on the street and in the locker room. An officer has too much of himself on the line to allow anything less than total dedication from fellow officers.

Setting personal standards by deed and example illustrate that an officer leaves little margin for anything less. Thereby establishing a moral high ground and identity with purpose.

I'm not saying you can't have fun in life. There is a time to laugh and a time to cry. I just think it proper to apply common sense. It is indeed unfortunate but some officers are completely void of that virtue. Always be aware of those around you.

DO NOT BECOME A MEMBER OF THE BLUE MINORITY. I look at fellow officers who only associate and socialize with other police officers and I feel sorry for them. There are far more good people in the community than bad. Being part of that minority establishes a foundation for the "us against them" mindset.

Police and public communication is the very heart of good police work. Obviously, the "us against them" approach is a barrier to that communication and the effectiveness of the department's mission.

The next logical step after the, "us against them" is double standard. "You can't do this but I can because I'm a police officer." Sorry Pal, this is very real, it does exist and should be identified and weeded out.

A badge is a symbol of public trust. That badge must be earned every hour, every day, every week, every month and every year until it is turned in for retirement. Some earn that trust every day and some ride that trust without ever doing a thing. Kick the slackers off the wagon until they earn the ride.

NEVER LIE. An officer must command respect. It sounds simple but it's not. That respect must be earned on a daily basis. It's all in the approach of being part of the community. Traditionally, a uniformed police office stands for what is morally right. Most young folks know that and from time to time will solicit answers to their most personal questions.

Most high school students are in a difficult period in their lives. They are constantly being pulled between what they know as right or wrong and what their peers expect from them. Don't make the mistake of writing their questions off as "kid stuff." Remember a lot of these "kids" are old enough to fight and die for our country.

The only approach is to answer their questions honestly. They might not like the answer, but it's an honest answer. Over time that honest answer builds trust and respect. Although, the answer might not have been the answer that person wanted to hear at that time, it left the impression that the uniform and officer stand on the moral high-ground. Remember, high school people are only a short time away from being fathers, mothers, taxpayers, and good citizens.

The Courtroom is where it all comes together. Once an officer establishes his integrity, court becomes "Let's Make A Deal Day."

New officers get really up tight about defense attorneys and DA's. The fact is, no attorney alive can change the facts of a case. The truth isn't going to change, no matter how it is framed.

A new officer may lose a case on a procedural error. That is part of the learning process. The important issue remains very clear, the Judge's quickly learn the truthfulness of the officers in their court. If an officer commands the respect of the judge, all the participants of that court, DA's, defense attorneys and the public get the message really quick. Remember, the officer is only as good as his word.

DON'T GET HUNG UP ON COURT SENTENCES. Too many officers fall into this trap. The officer's job is to enforce the law; that's it. The Judge's job is to impose sentence. Officers sometimes don't get the big picture that politics has a lot to do with sentencing. There are several factors that come into play, and they are the subjects of several books so I need not expound upon them here.

Politics remains the ugly and nasty form of crime that is socially acceptable in our society. It is the only stage where one person can savagely attack another and get away with it. It is indeed unfortunate that politics must enter into law enforcement but it does. Judges are appointed by Governors, Sheriffs are elected, Chiefs are appointed and some officers are hired because of their politics.

I always found one fact to hold true. One can always tell when a politician is lying; their lips are moving. That is the reason that a policeman's lot is not a happy one.

The officer in a courtroom doesn't have to consider the cost overrun at the County Jail, the case load of the DA's office, the political affiliation of the defense attorney, or a favor owed from a golf game. The cold hard facts are that the officer remains the constant professional. The saving grace is that "every dog has his day." Sooner or later, the officer will get the satisfaction of watching the frequent flyers get their just desserts.

THINK PROFESSIONAL and therefore be professional. Being a law enforcement officer is not a job, it is a way of life. The position demands total dedication. If you're not up to that commitment, law enforcement is not for you.

The term is: Squared Away! That's right, squared away in everything you do from dressing in that uniform everyday to keeping the cruiser shined inside and out. The officer and his/her Department are judged every day by what the public sees. That is a cold hard fact. A sloppy uniform, a dirty vehicle, poor posture, bad language, all contribute to the public's perception of you and your Department. An officer that respects him/herself, begets respect for the Department.

Hand shakes and greetings should always emit character. An officer should present character by demeanor. Respect for the officer, Department and the profession hinge on such little things. It is a good rule and gauge to view every introduction to a member of the public as if it were the first time that person ever spoke with a police officer. The impression the officer leaves will be a lasting one.

In the course of daily events, an officer learns many things about the lives of the people in the community. Keeping those facts is a trust. The true professional maintains a relationship with the public, never revealing that private information. The true professional always protects the dignity of the public.

It is often necessary to take a person's freedom away by placing him/her under arrest. That never gives the officer a right to attack that person's dignity. Experienced officers know that by allowing a person to retain their dignity, respect is mutual. Respect earns communication and information is the most important asset of a good police officer.

Be aware of where you are seen in public. Understand that the public is always watching. PAY for that cup of coffee. Insist on it, but always say thanks for the offer. Think about it, would an officer be offered a free cup of coffee if you weren't an officer? Did everyone in the coffee shop get the same offer? Taking that free cup of coffee would alienate the officer from every other customer in that shop.

LOYALTY is the most important and least understood attribute of a police officer. An officer's loyalty is NOT to any other officer, but to the Department and the Mission.

Each officer is commissioned to accomplish the mission of his/her Department. That commission is a very personal relationship with the Department. That Commission is about the officer being entrusted with the membership, goals and objectives of the Department.

The officer's true loyalty is to the Department. No friendship, working relationship or association should ever be allowed to detract from that obligation. An officer must realize that his personal commitment is of the highest order. Always work to be worthy of that commission.

So too; must an officer be ready to accept that other officers are not worthy of that commission. That very personal relationship should never be compromised by a misplaced loyalty to another officer, friend or not. A true friend within the profession will never compromise another officer's loyalty.

Upon this one fact there is no room for bad judgement. An officer must protect his commission and never allow his loyalty to become clouded.

There is only one place for a bad officer. That place is outside the door of law enforcement. Because an officer has so much of him/her self vested in the commission, there is no room for anyone less vested. Either they measure up or they don't. A good officer has the ability to separate professionalism and friendship. The two are not joined together by a uniform.

The order of loyalty is really quite simple. First, be loyal to yourself and your convictions. Know what your name stands for and be steadfast in your resolve. Never allow anyone, cop or civilian to stain your integrity.

That loyalty includes sharing your burden with your spouse. A loved one knows and understands. A good relationship is based on mutual respect. This is the first and most basic step toward stress management and always being the best you can be.

Secondly, be loyal to your Department and it's Mission. An officer must be proud of his/her Department. Support and protect your Department from ineptitude and complacency. An officer should never publicly criticize his/her Department and or another member of the Department.

If an officer finds it morally necessary to criticize a Department in public, he/she should first leave the Department. Utilize the structure within the Department first. Exhaust every avenue available to improve the Department from within.

This is the most predominant reason for high stress levels among officers. That fact will never change. Supervisors, command officers, and Chiefs become reticent to change and technology as retirement nears. Less senior officers identify their needs on the street but become stressed when leadership doesn't share the officer's priorities. Some philosopher said it best, "patience is a virtue."

YOU DON'T GET PAID TO COME IN SECOND. When an officer is challenged, either physically or mentally on the street, first place is all that counts. Be smarter than the average bear.

If an arrest must be effected, utilize whatever resources are available to bring about the correct moral and legal end to the situation. Weigh your options, have a plan of action and resolve the situation professionally.

Don't let your mouth overload your ass. Desecration is the better part of valor. Calm and quite resolve will always put the officer in first place. All poor officers are generally void of one important virtue; common sense.

There is no urgency to arrest anyone. "Every dog has his day." Hey, some days it hard to find a bone and other days it's all steak and gravy. Police work is like the new nutrition plan, small meals and often. Little bits of information add up.

KEEP YOUR MOUTH SHUT ABOUT THE DEPARTMENT. Guard against idle conversation between officers at a local coffee shop. People are listening. A good police officer comes out of one of those places with information. A bad officer, runs his mouth to impress the waitress and the result is that it isn't long before the whole community knows the Department's business and respect for the Department is in the dumpster.

Being a good conversationalist is very important to an officer's effectiveness in the community. Leading questions such as: Where are you from? Have we met? What's going on? Do you live on ____ street? All play a role in inviting the public to talk with an officer. It affords the public a more intimate one on one opportunity to get to know the officer. Tons of good information and community relations come from that type of conversation in the coffee shop.

PROTECT YOUR FAMILY LIFE. Time demands on an officer are sometimes overwhelming. The family comes first. Children are only young once. Sharing their accomplishments in life is important. The officer who puts his/her career first usually has a disastrous homelife.

It's great to have the neighborhood kids look up to an officer, but it's more important for the officer's kids to look up to him/her. Love and support are right a home. Make the most of it.

SO, YOU WANT TO BE A COP?
EXPECT TO BE POOR, OVER WORKED, UNAPPRECIATED AND FORGOTTEN ONE DAY AFTER RETIREMENT.

You must be number than a pounded thumb!

I wish you all the success in the world. Hey, stop by and visit us old dinosaurs once in a while. We'll enjoy the company and you can see just how you're going to look when it's over. RIDDEN HARD AND PUT AWAY WET!

A
SPECIAL NOTE

It wasn't a cold day in hell when I first met Paul Main, it was a freezing day in Maine. It was Deputy Main that had requested that I conduct a class on criminal personalities for his department and several surrounding police departments. This meeting is the meeting that began a very close and personal friendship that has spanned over twenty years. It has endured two marriages, career changes, retirements, new jobs and numerous pig roasts.

Throughout this time I have always appreciated and respected Paul's wit, humor, intelligence and his ability to immediately size up and act upon a situation. His ability to accurately assess another person's personality is absolutely uncanny.

I am humbled, honored and proud to call Paul Main my friend.

James M. Moores
Special Agent, F.B.I (retired)

www.ingramcontent.com/pod-product-compliance
Lightning Source LLC
Chambersburg PA
CBHW020310290526
45784CB00003B/1456